www.wadsworth.com

wadsworth.com is the World Wide Web site
for Wadsworth and is your direct source
to dozens of online resources.

At wadsworth.com you can find out about
supplements, demonstration software, and
student resources. You can also send e-mail to
many of our authors and preview new publications
and exciting new technologies.

wadsworth.com
Changing the way the world learns®

From the Wadsworth Series in Mass Communication and Journalism

General Mass Communication

Biagi, *Media/Impact: An Introduction to Mass Media*, 4th Ed.
Biagi, *Media/Reader: Perspectives on Media Industries, Effects, and Issues*, 3rd Ed.
Day, *Ethics in Media Communications; Cases and Controversies*, 3rd Ed.
Fortner, *International Communications: History, Conflict, and Control of the Global Metropolis*
Jamieson and Campbell, *The Interplay of Influence*, 4th Ed.
Lester, *Visual Communication*, 2nd Ed.
Lont, *Women and Media: Content, Careers, and Criticism*
Straubhaar and LaRose, *Media Now: Communications Media in the Information Age*, 2nd Ed.
Surette, *Media, Crime, and Criminal Justice: Images and Realities*, 2nd Ed.
Whetmore, *Mediamerica, Mediaworld: Form, Content, and Consequence of Mass Communication*, Updated 5th Ed.
Zelezny, *Communications Law: Liberties, Restraints, and the Modern Media*, 2nd Ed.

Journalism

Bowles and Borden, *Creative Editing for Print Media*, 3rd Ed.
Hilliard, *Writing for Television, Radio & New Media*, 7th Ed.
Kessler and McDonald, *The Search: Information Gathering for the Mass Media*
Kessler and McDonald, *When Words Collide*, 5th Ed.
Klement and Matalene, *Telling Stories/Taking Risks: Journalism Writing at the Century's Edge*
Parrish, *Photojournalism: An Introduction*
Rich, *Writing and Reporting News: A Coaching Method*, 3rd Ed.
Rich, *Workbook for Writing and Reporting News*, 3rd Ed.

Photojournalism and Photography

Parrish, *Photojournalism: An Introduction*
Rosen and DeVries, *Introduction to Photography*, 4th Ed.

Public Relations and Advertising

Hendrix, *Public Relations Cases*, 4th Ed.
Jewler and Drewniany, *Creative Strategy in Advertising*, 6th Ed.
Marlow, *Electronic Public Relations*
Mueller, *International Advertising: Communicating Across Cultures*
Newsom and Carrell, *Public Relations Writing: Form and Style*, 5th Ed.
Newsom, Turk, and Kruckeberg, *This Is PR: The Realities of Public Relations*, 7th Ed.
Sivulka, *Soap, Sex, and Cigarettes: A Cultural History of American Advertising*
Woods, *Advertising and Marketing to the New Majority: A Case Study Approach*

Research and Theory

Babbie, *The Practice of Social Research*, 8th Ed.
Baran and Davis, *Mass Communication Theory: Foundations, Ferment, and Future*, 2nd Ed.
Rubenstein, *Surveying Public Opinion*
Rubin, Rubin, and Piele, *Communication Research: Strategies and Sources*, 5th Ed.
Wimmer and Dominick, *Mass Media Research: An Introduction*, 6th Ed.

WHEN WORDS COLLIDE

A Media Writer's Guide to Grammar and Style

FIFTH EDITION

Lauren Kessler
UNIVERSITY OF OREGON

Duncan McDonald
UNIVERSITY OF OREGON

Wadsworth
Thomson Learning™

Australia · Canada · Denmark · Japan · Mexico · New Zealand · Phillippines
Puerto Rico · Singapore · South Africa · Spain · United Kingdom · United States

Mass Communication and Journalism
  Editor: Karen Austin
Executive Editor: Deirdre Cavanaugh
Assistant Editor: Ryan E. Vesely
Editorial Assistant: Dory Schaeffer
Project Editor: Cathy Linberg
Print Buyer: Mary Noel
Permissions Editor: Robert M. Kauser

Production Service: nSight
Text Designer: Wendy LaChance/By Design
Copy Editor: Theresa Horton
Compositor: Tara Murray, nSight
Cover Designer: Delgado Design, Inc.
Printer: Transcontinental Printing

Printed in Canada
       6 7 03 02

For permission to use material from
this text, contact us:
  web: www.thomsonrights.com
  fax: 1-800-730-2215
  phone: 1-800-730-2214

Wadsworth/Thomson Learning
10 Davis Drive
Belmont, CA 94002-3098
USA
www.wadsworth.com

International Headquarters
Thomson Learning
290 Harbor Drive, 2nd Floor
Stamford, CT 06902-7477
USA

UK/Europe/Middle East
Thomson Learning
Berkshire House
168-173 High Holborn
London WC1V 7AA
United Kingdom

Asia
Thomson Learning
60 Albert Street #15-01
Albert Complex
Singapore 189969

Canada
Nelson/Thomson Learning
1120 Birchmount Road
Scarborough, Ontario M1K 5G4
Canada

Library of Congress Cataloging-in-Publication Data
Kessler, Lauren.
    When words collide: a media writer's guide to grammar and style/
Lauren Kessler, Duncan McDonald. —5th ed.
        p.   cm.
    Includes index.
    ISBN 0-534-56133-0
    1. English language—Grammar. 2. Journalism—Style manuals.
    3. Journalism—Authorship. 4. Mass media—Authorship.
I. McDonald, Duncan. II. Title.
PE1112.K435 2000
808'.042—dc21
Instructor's Edition ISBN 0-534-56136-5   99-35245

CONTENTS

PREFACE

Welcome to the fifth edition of "When Words Collide." This book is new to you, but it has been a part of our lives for almost 15 years. In that time, we have worked with hundreds of writers, watching both novices and veterans wrestle their ideas into sentences, mold language to meaning and write pieces they—and we—are proud of. Whether they were news stories or personal essays, press releases or print ads, magazine features or cyberjournalism, all this writing had one thing in common. That's right. You guessed it: careful attention to the architecture of language, solid fundamentals—in other words, good grammar.

We want you to know that writers wrote this book. We are two people who massage words every day, who, we must admit, occasionally page through our own book to help answer a particularly tricky grammatical question. As productive writers ourselves, we are close to the issues all writers struggle with regardless of how many years or how many stories have gone by. "When Words Collide" is written from that perspective: writer to writer.

The construction of language is a powerful act through which we humans learn and grow. Speaking and writing, we establish relationships, conduct business, exchange information and express emotions. As writers, we do even more: We use the language to make history, to make art. When we are successful, it is because we select and use language carefully, purposefully, artfully and based on shared, logical understanding. We become masters at arranging language in coherent patterns. Grammar, this arrangement, is at the heart of effective communication.

That's why we wrote the very first edition of "When Words Collide," and that's why we now offer you this newest edition, the fifth. We want to help you use the language well.

We think this new edition is even stronger and more useful than its predecessors. We've expanded and clarified, edited and polished. We've added sections, examples and entries. We've brought the challenges and insights from our own writing lives to these pages, hoping this book will find a place by your side as you learn and perfect your craft.

ACKNOWLEDGMENTS

We thank the following reviewers for their ideas and comments: For this edition they were: Mike Henderson, University of Washington; Kay Phillips, University of North Carolina-Chapel Hill; Mary Quigly, New York University; Paula Renfro, Southwest Texas State University; and John Allman, University of Minnesota. For previous editions they were: Carrie Carr, Baylor University; Kevin Hall, Florida International University; David Maloof, Boston University; Kathy McAdams, University of Maryland; Nancy Mitchell, University of Nebraska; and Andrea Nichols, Baylor University. We also thank the many teachers around the country who have class-tested "When Words Collide" and written to us about their experiences. And we thank—and would like to recognize—the thousands of students who have struggled with the complexities of the English language on the road to becoming professional writers. "When Words Collide" is dedicated to them and to our families—Tom, Jackson, Zane and Elizabeth, and Jane and Vanessa.

PART 1

Understanding Grammar and Style

CHAPTER 1

What You Don't Know *Will* Hurt You

So, just hearing the word "grammar" makes you wince. Or get a headache. Or want to take a long nap. We know. We understand. Grammar has a bad rap. You think it's a litany of complex rules meant to confuse you. You think it will inhibit your creativity. You think only fussy, bespectacled high school English teachers care about it.

You're wrong.

Listen: You're a writer, or want to be. Words are your tools, and grammar is the instruction manual that helps you use them. Grammar doesn't inhibit style. *It makes style possible.* More than that, grammar makes communication possible. Without the shared conventions of grammar, without the structure it creates and the patterns it plots, we could not speak to each other across time and space. Grammar is the writers' touchstone, our ritual. It binds us together whether we write journal entries or journalism, haiku or press releases, whether our book is number one on the *New York Times* best seller list, or we have just registered for our first writing class.

Not convinced yet? You still don't want to believe that grammar—like broccoli, like a brisk 30-minute walk—is good for you, essential for your writerly health? "I never learned grammar in school, but it hasn't hurt me yet," you say. "I can always write around what I don't know," you insist. "Hey, it's the ideas that count, not the grammar," you declare.

You're wrong. Grammar is fundamental to good writing.

Consider this comment from journalist, essayist, novelist and screenwriter Joan Didion, one of the finest prose stylists writing today: "All I know about grammar is its infinite power," she writes. "To shift the structure of a sentence alters the meaning of that sentence, as definitely and inflexibly as the position of a camera alters the meaning of the object photographed. Many people know about cameras today, but not so many know about sentences."

But we *must* know about sentences, about phrases, clauses, voices, tenses, singulars, plurals—all the patterns and constructions that make our language work. Language is how we spread ideas and information throughout society. The information we have to communicate as writers may be complex; the ideas may be challenging. The message will have to compete with countless distractions for the attention of the audience. This puts a tremendous burden on the language: It must be crisp and clear, easy to understand, inviting. It must carry the ideas effortlessly, even gracefully. It must enhance meaning. It must communicate tone and nuance, color and texture, sound and rhythm. But to do all this, the language must be—before all else—correct. Correctness hinges on knowing grammar, the guidelines that help us select, link and order words.

GRAMMAR IS IN THE EYES

All languages depend on rules of grammar, although these conventions may not be entirely evident to outsiders. Nonstandard English, the language as it is sometimes spoken in inner-city neighborhoods, may defy many of the rules of conventional English, but it has rules and patterns of its own, linguistic conventions that guide its use. So too does sign language, where grammar occurs in the eyes, the brows, the tilt of the head, the lips. Just as sentence construction communicates meaning in written English, a tucked chin, narrowed eyes or raised shoulders act as grammatical signposts in the language of the deaf. Even "baby talk" has its own simple grammar ("Me want milk.").

Face it: Grammar is everywhere.

Centuries ago, grammar meant far more than the architecture of language. In classical Greek and Latin, the word *grammar* meant the study of the entire field of literature. In the Middle Ages, *grammatica* was more narrowly defined as the knowledge or study of Latin, but the word slowly became synonymous with learning in general. To know *grammatica* was to be privy to all the knowledge of the learned class, which at the time included both magic and astrology. In fact, grammar (or various corruptions of the word) was sometimes used as a name for these occult sciences. The word *glamour*—which originally meant magic, enchantment and spell and has come to mean alluring charm—is a form of the word *grammar*.

Grammar is, in a real sense, still the study of magic. As any reader who has been transported by the written word knows, a sentence can be enchanting. But as any writer who has struggled with words realizes, there is little sleight of hand involved. The product may be magical, but the process is hard work.

THE WRITER AS ARTISAN

Consider writing as a craft, like carpentry. Just as a builder of fine furniture does not attempt to construct an oak cabinet using a dull saw and rusty nails, so too a writer cannot create a memorable passage using clichés and clumsy constructions. Artisans care about—and for—the tools of their trade, just as writers must. Think of learning grammar as learning how to use the right tool for the job.

Artisans have their self-respect tied to the quality of their craft. A skilled woodworker, for example, is meticulous about the quality and grain of the wood, the grade of the sandpaper, the luster of the finish. This care, this craftsmanship, far exceeds what is required to produce an adequate, serviceable cabinet. To approach writing this way, as a craft, is to go beyond correctness, beyond the adequate and toward the memorable.

Tom Paine, the Revolutionary War journalist, could have written

Men's souls are tried by these times

or

These times are trying to men's souls.

But he was an artisan, a wordsmith. He wanted to do more than produce an adequate, usable sentence. He wanted drama, rhythm and cadence. Like the master woodworker, he knew the tools of his craft and took great pride in using them well. He wrote

These are the times that try men's souls

and more than 200 years have not diminished the power and grace of that sentence.

Diverse crafts from writing to woodworking have the same requirements: self-discipline, knowledge of the medium and its tools, an ability to solve problems and pride in one's work. The first step to craftsmanship in writing is mastery of grammar. But that doesn't mean learning rules in a vacuum. Writers serious about their craft learn the structure of language by using it—writing—and by studying how others use it—reading.

THE WRITER AS ARTIST

Perhaps you would rather think of yourself as artist than artisan. Perhaps to you, writing goes beyond craft to art. It can, and does. But artists, too, pay particular attention to fundamentals, to the basic tools they will use to create their art. The painter studies color; the musician learns the scales; the actor takes classes in voice control and body movement. These fundamentals are not the art itself, just as grammar is not writing, but they are the path to mastery. Whether you consider writing an art or a craft or a bit of both, it is clear that you need to start with and build from the basics.

Artists, as we're sure you've noticed, occasionally break the rules to purposefully, even gleefully, defy the conventions of their own medium. Writers do this too. Think of William Faulkner's 100-plus-word sentences, grammatical run-ons that make you breathless and dizzy while they transport you to a world that exists only in the author's imagination. Note that the first paragraph in this chapter contains two fragments, incomplete constructions considered grammatical errors. We did that on purpose, not because we didn't know how to write a complete sentence. We broke the full-sentence rule to create a punchy, emphatic introduction that we hoped would grab your attention. Some rules can be broken to create special effects. But they must be *known* before they can be flouted.

MAKING MISTAKES

What is exciting and challenging about learning to write well is that it is a lifelong process. Throughout our lives as writers we will grow, we will change and, inevitably, we will make mistakes: judgments miscalled, questions unasked and language misused. Errors can be disheartening, not to mention embarrassing.

Grammatical errors are particularly dangerous to the professional lives of writers. "If I see a misspelled word on a resume or a grammatical error, I look no further. I immediately disqualify the applicant," says the personnel director of a large company. "We look at how much attention a person pays to detail," says the vice president of a major advertising firm. "Things like grammar, spelling and mechanics mean a lot to us. We figure, if the person can't accomplish these things, how can we expect him or her to move on to bigger jobs?" Says a newspaper editor, "If I find grammatical and mechanical errors in the first paragraph, I stop reading. If a person can't use grammar correctly, it says either of two things to me—lack of intelligence or extreme sloppiness. Either way, it's not the person I want writing for me."

But mistakes do happen. It is precisely because professional writers know this—and understand the unpleasant consequences of making errors publicly—that they take *editing* so seriously. They begin with a solid understanding of the language and then they edit, edit, edit. The misspelled word, the misplaced modifier, the lack of parallelism, the shift in voice, all the little errors that can creep into writing never make it past the editing process. It is here experienced writers turn their uncertain, sometimes ragged prose into the polished material they can proudly present to their audience.

WHAT YOU DON'T KNOW . . .

What you don't know *will* hurt you. It will hurt the clarity of your writing, the understanding and respect of your audience, even your ability to land a job in the first place. What is it you don't know? Let's consider ten of the most common grammatical mistakes and how knowledge of the language (and reading this book) can help you avoid them.

Mistake #1: Thinking you don't have to know grammar to write well. After reading this far, you certainly won't make this mistake again, will you?

Mistake #2: Subjects and verbs that don't agree. For a sentence to be grammatically correct and clearly communicative, a verb must agree with the intended number of its subject. That sounds simple, as in: *The book* (singular subject) *is* (singular verb) *in the library* or *The books* (plural subject) *are* (plural verb) *on the reading list*. But it gets complicated when you're not quite sure what the subject is. There may be a number of nouns and pronouns in the sentence. Which is the true subject? There may be confusion about the intended number of the verb. *Five thousand dollars*, as a subject, looks plural but acts singular; *Everyone* clearly implies the plural but acts as a singular subject. To sort this all out, you need to know the parts of speech (Chapter 2), the parts of a sentence (Chapter 3) and the guidelines for agreement (Chapter 4).

Mistake #3: Subjects and pronouns that don't agree. To communicate crisply and clearly, sentences must have internal harmony. Just as subjects and verbs must agree, so too must subjects and their pronouns. Adhering to this straightforward rule depends on your ability to identify the subject, recognize its number and choose a corresponding pronoun. This can be simple, as in: *The books* (plural subject) *and their* (plural pronoun) *authors.* Or it can be tougher, as in: *Everyone should remain in (their/his or her) seat* or *The team made (their/its) way to the locker room.* But if you understand parts of speech (Chapter 2) and the guidelines for agreement (Chapter 4), you should be able to avoid this pitfall.

Mistake #4: Lack of parallelism. To be both coherent and forceful, a sentence must have parallel structure; that is, its elements must be in balance. A construction like: *I came. I saw. I conquered* is powerful because it sets out three ideas in three parallel grammatical structures (pronoun–past-tense verb). Consider the same idea expressed this way: *I came. I looked over everything. The enemy was conquered by my armies.* That's lack of parallelism. That's bad writing. You have to know the parts of speech (Chapter 2) to understand the concept of parallelism, and you must see parallelism as a form of agreement (Chapter 4).

Mistake #5: Confusing who and whom. *Who/Whom* did the president name to his cabinet? She voted for *whoever/whomever* endorsed the treaty. The judge *who/whom* tried the case refused to speak with reporters. Confused? You won't be once you understand the nominative and objective cases (Chapter 5).

Mistake #6: Confusing that and which. Did you think these two words were interchangeable, as in: *The readership poll that/which the magazine commissioned helped shape editorial policy.* Well, they aren't. *That* is used to introduce material that restricts the meaning of the noun; *which* is used to elaborate on meaning. If you know about relative pronouns (Chapter 2) and the role of phrases and clauses in a sentence (Chapter 3), you will use these words correctly.

Mistake #7: Confusing possessives and contractions. That's a fancy way of saying that *your* (possessive) and *you're* (contraction) are not interchangeable. They are meant to perform very different tasks in a sentence. *Their* and *they're, whose* and *who's, its* and *it's* may sound the same, but they do not perform the same grammatical functions. Learning parts of speech (Chapter 2) and case (Chapter 5) will end the confusion.

Mistake #8: Dangling and misplacing modifiers. A misplaced modifier (a word, phrase or clause) does not point clearly and directly to what it is supposed to modify. A modifier "dangles" when what it is supposed to modify is not part of the sentence. Both grammatical errors seriously compromise clarity of meaning. If you understand parts of speech (Chapter 2) and parts of the sentence (Chapter 3), then this clarity, conciseness and coherence issue (Chapter 9) will make sense.

Mistake #9: Misusing commas. Some novice writers just don't take commas seriously enough, sprinkling them throughout sentences like decoration, figuring "when in doubt, put one in." But commas have specific functions in a sentence, as do all pieces of punctuation. In addition to generally overusing commas, writers frequently fall prey to two other comma errors. One is neglecting to use a comma to separate two independent clauses linked by a coordinating conjunction. The other, ironically, is using only a comma when trying to link two independent clauses (known as the "comma splice" error). If some of this terminology is foreign to you, it won't be after you read about parts of speech (Chapter 2), the sentence (Chapter 3) and punctuation (Chapter 7).

Mistake #10: The dreaded passive voice. Do you know what the passive voice is? You will, after reading Chapter 6. It is one of the surest ways to suck the life out of a sentence and construct stilted, falsely formal or bureaucratic prose. Although technically passive voice construction is not a grammatical error and although there are a few defensible reasons for using this construction, most passive voice sentences are not written knowingly or purposefully. Both the clarity (Chapter 9) and liveliness (Chapter 10) of writing are at stake.

All these grammatical hazards—we could list hundreds more— may seem daunting. Don't be daunted. Be respectful. Understand that language is alive, complex, fascinating—and full of potential pitfalls. That doesn't mean you should be intimidated. It means you should be careful. It means you should learn the tools of your trade. It means you should study the fundamentals and build a writing life from this firm foundation. "When Words Collide" can help.

WHEN WORDS COLLIDE

When words collide, they can collide like trucks on the highway, all bent fenders and shattered glass. Or they can collide like atoms of uranium, releasing power and force. Grammatical errors cause words to collide with disastrous results. Grammatical mastery—part of the craftsmanship and artistry of writers who care about their work—causes words to collide in a creative burst of energy.

The study of grammar is more than the study of the rules and regulations that give order and structure to the language. The study of grammar is the key to the power of words. Read on. Write on.

CHAPTER 2

Parts of Speech

<u>Breathe</u> easily.

<u>Open</u> your mind.

<u>Relax</u>!

This is the page where you start your march to understanding sentence construction. It's where you begin to identify and acquire the tools to construct your thoughts correctly and clearly.

This is where you will begin the "dance of words" that will give voice to your ideas.

The key is parts of speech—the building blocks of a sentence. It may not be romantic to think of the wonders of human communication as construction materials, but it's not a bad learning device. It is true that in our everyday use of language, we rarely give a thought to the complex architecture of our communication. We construct our two-line message at the bottom of a greeting card or our rapid-fire response to an e-mail without thinking about the critical functions of single words in the assembly of thought. And yet, most of us would claim that we have a workable, intuitive sense for how to make that construction correct.

We're going beyond that here, in our belief that good writers need more than good intuition. Good writers need solid mechanics to give integrity to their creative structures.

Let's get right into it.

The first three sentences in this chapter began with verbs. In fact, the third sentence was a verb, all by its lonesome. We began this way because all writing begins with the verb. Our ideas simply can't get moving without them. They provide power and force to our expression. And what of the adjective? It provides description and detail. The conjunction? It is a bridge for thoughts that need connection. Indeed, the "use categories" that constitute our seven basic *parts of speech* are central to the construction of our language. (OK, technically there are eight, but we're really not sure how the interjection got on the team!)

Unless we understand how to use parts of speech, we cannot create effective, sustainable thought. It's unfortunate, then, that the very term "parts of speech" can evoke nightmarish visions of diagramming sentences or of creating "sentence trees." We'll not offer up such a horror, but we hope you will soon understand the relationship between comprehending parts of speech, mastering grammar and writing well.

Consider these sentences. The seven parts of speech that are underlined show how these parts interact to make these thoughts flow coherently:

He   hates   mistakes.
(pronoun as   (verb, directs   (noun, receives action)
subject   action)
of sentence)

He   really   hates   silly   mistakes.
(pron.)   (adverb, helps   (verb)   (adjective,   (noun)
           characterize verb)   characterizes
                                         noun)

He   really   hates   silly   mistakes,
(pron.)   (adv.)   (verb)   (adjec.)   (noun)

but   he believes we can learn from them.
(conjunction,   (preposition, connects word or
joins two clauses)   phrase to show relationship)

MORE REASONS, PLEASE!

So, how will a solid understanding of parts of speech help you master the challenges of grammar? Here are several examples:

- Proper recognition of a verb helps you distinguish a phrase from a clause. As Chapter 3 will point out, a phrase, which is an important part of sentence construction, does not contain a verb. Therefore, a construction such as

The dark, windswept ocean sky

is neither a clause nor a complete sentence; it is a phrase composed of four adjectives and one noun. It has no verb and cannot stand alone. It becomes a clause with the insertion of an "action" word:

The dark, windswept ocean sky <u>warned</u> us of a rainy day.

Now we have a clause, and because this one can stand independently, it is a complete thought. We have a verb. We have a sentence.

- Proper recognition of a sentence subject will prevent errors in subject-verb agreement. Not all nouns are subjects of a sentence, and the proximity of a noun to a verb is not the main determinant of whether the verb is singular or plural, as in this example:

Her <u>decision</u> about the four criminal <u>complaints</u>
(noun—subj.)   (also a noun, but not the subj.)
<u>has been supported</u> in the press.
(verb—singular)

Inexperienced writers could be fooled about the plural noun *complaints*, thinking that it might be the subject of the sentence and therefore require a plural verb. However, the seasoned writer properly notes that *about* is a preposition and that the noun following it is called the *object* of a preposition. You'll have a complete explanation of that starting on page 34.

- Proper recognition of how a pronoun functions in a sentence will help you make the correct selection of subjective or objective case for that pronoun. For example, a decision about the use of *I* or *me* in the following sentence turns on understanding what both prepositions and pronouns do:

<u>Between</u> you and <u>me</u>, I'm really going to enjoy this book!
(prep.,   (pron., in objective case)
requires object)

Get the point? These are just a few of the many good examples of why understanding parts of speech is critical to understanding grammar.

Now we'll examine each part of speech to understand its role in sentence construction. Let's start at the heart—or engine—of the sentence: the verb.

VERBS

All of the energy of a sentence springs from its "reactor core"—the *verb*. Its name is derived from the Latin *verbum,* or *word.* Consider that word as a messenger of action or being, one that delivers the power of meaning. Without the power of a verb, a sentence is a hollow, impotent shell that cannot deliver a complete thought. Put another way: no verb, no sentence.

Verbs have such power that one verb, standing alone, can express a complete thought, as in

Stop!
(The subject, *you* [a pronoun], is understood.)

Lacking a verb, these words are nothing but a static label:

A stop sign

Verbs explain what happened:

Three people <u>died</u> last night when a four-alarm fire <u>roared</u> through a downtown factory recently <u>cited</u> for improper storage of flammable materials.

Try reading this sentence without the underlined verbs. Nothing happens. It makes no sense.

VERB FUNCTIONS

Verbs aren't always dynamic. In addition to performing an action, they can also demonstrate a location or position as well as indicating a particular state of being. Here are some examples:

• The "action" (or transitive) verb

The winter's first blizzard <u>hit</u> the city with unforgiving fury.

• The active but intransitive verb (without a receiver of an action)

The blizzard <u>slammed</u> into the city without warning.
(As the section on intransitive verbs will show, these verbs don't answer the question *what,* as do the transitive verbs. However, they "report" on the action of the sentence subject, rather than having the subject perform that action.)

- The linking verb, to indicate a state of being

The city <u>was</u> paralyzed by the sudden blizzard.
(The verb helps link the noun *city* with the adjective *paralyzed* to reflect a state of being.)

VERB FORMS

1. Transitive verbs. These are the "action" verbs with the most powerful engines—they move the action directly from the sentence subject to the object (which is why the noun that receives the action is called a *direct object*). So in this sentence

The tidal wave <u>crushed</u> the coastal village
(transitive verb)

we have action (*crushed*) being performed by the "actor" *tidal wave* (the sentence subject, a noun) to the recipient *coastal village* (another noun, appropriately called a direct object in this construction). The alignment of subject–verb–direct object is a key to proper identification of a transitive verb construction.

Identifying transitive verbs can be a great aid in two areas of your writing: proper selection of pronoun case (discussed at length starting on p. 26) and avoiding the use of passive voice (p. 85). Let's examine these two areas briefly to make the point about the work of the transitive verb.

<u>Whom</u> did the <u>legislature</u> <u>name</u> as speaker?
(direct obj.)   (subj.)   (trans. verb)

In this sentence, which you can mentally readjust to read

The <u>legislature</u> <u>did name</u>   <u>whom</u> as speaker
(subj.)   (trans. verb) (dir. obj.)

you can see the flow of action from subject to object through the action of naming. When the pronoun *who* is placed in the role of direct object, it must change its form to the objective case, as *whom*. When you are alert to the presence of a transitive verb, you are also on watch for its object.

Passive voice is generally a weak construction; it deflects any action away from the subject of a sentence and never requires a direct object. For that reason, a transitive verb could not exist in a passive voice construction. Here is an example:

The coastal village <u>was crushed</u> by the tidal wave.
(intransitive verb)

As you can see, the subject (*village*) performs no action; it has an action performed on it. This is a good point at which to move on to the intransitive verb, which requires no object.

2. Intransitive verbs. Although these verbs *never* take a direct object, they can provide action and give a sense of location or being. The verb may be followed by a phrase that tells us *where* or *how,* but never *what,* as in

The suspect <u>crouched</u> in the alley as police arrived.
(intrans. verb)

Note that there is no direct object following *crouched*; what follows it is a prepositional phrase (see p. 35). *In the alley* provides helpful information as to location but does not complete an action.

This next sentence also contains an intransitive verb:

Bluto <u>scored</u> at will against Transylvania State.
(intrans. verb)

Instead of having this sentence receive the action of its verb (*scored*), it merely answers *how* and *where.* Bluto clearly performs some action, but there is no direct receiver of his action—unless you create this transitive construction:

Bluto <u>hurt</u> Transylvania State with his three-pointers.
(trans. verb)

See the difference?

In addition to dealing properly with passive voice constructions, understanding the difference between transitive and intransitive verb forms can eliminate errors in selecting the correct verb from such troublesome pairs as *lay/lie, set/sit* and *raise/rise.* The first verb in these combinations is transitive; it requires an object that answers the question *what.*

Lay the <u>book</u> on the table.

Please set your <u>clocks</u> back tonight.

The company will raise its <u>insurance rates</u>.

(The direct objects are underlined.)

On the other hand, verbs such as *lie, sit* and *rise* are intransitive.

<u>Lie</u> down and get some rest.

<u>Sit</u> in this chair, please.

I will <u>rise</u> early tomorrow.

Do you see any direct objects in the three preceding sentences? It's simple and true: Recognizing the difference between transitive and intransitive verbs can eliminate most verb choice problems.

3. Linking verbs. This verb form, frequently a derivative of *to be,* implies a state of being rather than expressing any direct action. The main function of this verb form is to connect the sentence subject with a modifier of sorts to help describe that state of being, as in these two sentences:

The <u>victim</u>   <u>was</u>   <u>comatose</u> when police found him.
  (subj.)   (linking   (adj.)
        verb)

Before collapsing, the judge said that <u>he</u>   <u>felt</u>   <u>ill</u>.
                             (subj.) (l.v.) (adj.)

Clearly, these verbs transmit conditions, not actions. For this reason, we say that they link a state or quality to a subject. Thus words like *comatose* and *ill* are officially termed *predicate adjectives* because with the help of the verb, they describe some quality of the subject. However, a noun (*predicate nominative*) can also follow a linking verb, as in

"The Joy of Cooking" <u>is</u> a well-known <u>book</u>.
             (l.v.)   (noun)

Note that with the use of a noun, a linking verb can answer the question *what.*

Verbs other than forms of *to be* (*am, is, are, was, were*) also can be linking verbs. They include: *appear, become, feel, get, look, remain, seem, smell, sound, taste.*

Some verbs can be used with all verb forms. The relationship of words surrounding those verbs provide the key to understanding the function of those verbs:

"I smell a rat here," the committee told the special prosecutor.
(*Smell* is a transitive verb. Direct object (*rat*) follows. It answers *what* and does not indicate location or a quality.)

The arson investigator thought the sofa smelled like kerosene.
(*Smelled* is an intransitive verb. It has no object for its action. What follows the verb is a prepositional phrase, *like kerosene,* and it answers *how.*)

The bullet-riddled corpse smelled bad.
(In this sentence, *smelled* is a linking verb. The verb links the quality *bad,* an adjective, to the subject noun *corpse,* which is why *bad* would be called a predicate adjective in this construction.)

Several other aspects of verbs also need to be discussed: tense, principal parts, mood and verbals.

VERB TENSE

Verbs help us relate a sense of history—that is, they can be formed to indicate the past, present and the future, as well as a variety of more complicated mixtures of time. Here's a brief sampler, just to make you familiar with the range. We'll do it with the same content topic.

Abraham Lincoln is our president.
(*Present tense* of verb—to be accurate, this sentence had to have been written between 1861 and 1865.)

Abraham Lincoln was our 16th president.
(*Past tense* of verb—this sentence had to be written after April 14, 1865, when President Lincoln was assassinated.)

One day soon, "Honest Abe" will be our president.
(*Future tense* of verb—this sentence could have been written in 1850, when Mr. Lincoln was toiling as lawyer and state politician in Illinois.)

We also use a host of "perfect tenses" in our writing, to indicate a past, continuing or future action. Another sampler:

Honest Abe <u>has been</u> a great president.
(This is called *present perfect*. The action is ongoing; obviously, some of it has happened, but at this point—let's say 1864—the presidency is not over.)

At the time of his assassination, Abraham Lincoln <u>had been</u> an embattled leader whose presidency <u>had been ravaged</u> by the Civil War.
(This is called *past perfect*. We are dealing with the past tense, but this sentence reflects an action that occurred prior to some other action in the past, such as the subsequent inauguration of Andrew Johnson.)

There are other forms of "perfect" constructions, but we hope you get the idea from this brief review (and that you enjoyed the history lesson!).

PRINCIPAL PARTS OF VERBS

As you can tell from the previous section, a verb will change both spelling and meaning when its tense changes. One way of understanding these changes is to examine what is called the *principal parts* of those verbs.

All verbs start off with a basic form, which is essentially the present tense of that verb, or how it is shown in most dictionaries. If you add in the past tense and then a construction called the *past participle,* you have every possible form in which the verb will be used. Consider, for example, the verb *grow:* The present tense is *grow,* the past tense is *grew,* the past participle is *grown.* So, with these three verb forms, you can write

She <u>grows</u> alfalfa.

She <u>grew</u> alfala.

She <u>will grow</u> alfalfa.

She <u>has grown</u> alfalfa.

She <u>had grown</u> alfalfa during the Great Depression but switched to corn when Franklin Roosevelt was elected.

Verbs vary in how they change spelling to reflect their form. If a verb is *regular*, the past tense and past participle are created simply by adding -*ed* to the present form, as in

The politicians <u>intend</u> to answer the voters' charges.

The politicians <u>intended</u> to answer the charges, but they were jailed before they had the opportunity to respond.

Irregular verbs are so labeled because their change from present to past and to past participle is, well, different. Consider, for example, these verbs:

Present	Past	Past Perfect
begin	began	begun
choose	chose	chosen
drink	drank	drunk
lie	lay	lain
rise	rose	risen
see	saw	seen
spring	sprang	sprung
wake	woke	waked

Fortunately, your dictionary is a valuable (and handy, we hope) resource for parsing a verb's principal parts. A quick check of *swear,* for example, shows *swore* and *sworn* as past tense and past participle, respectively. An answer is always close if you have the right reference materials.

VERB MOODS

Our verbs carry *moods*, which can vary from direct statements of fact to possibilities or conjecture. These moods are labeled *indicative, imperative* and *subjunctive*. We'll focus mainly on the subjunctive here, as selection of the verb form can seem improper at first. However, let's give an example of both the indicative and imperative moods:

• Indicative. This mood specifies either a fact or a question, as in

The Congressional hearings were shocking.

Did you think the hearings were shocking?

- Imperative. This mood is more directive; it can even command, as in

Stop these hearings immediately!
(Note: The subject, *you*, is understood.)

- Subjunctive. When a sentence is written to express a wish, desire or a statement that is contrary to fact, or when it presents a recommendation, it employs a verb in the subjunctive mood. It requires what may seem like an unusual change in verb form, which uses a plural form of a verb or in some cases, a switch from *is/are* to *be*. Some examples, beginning with the Jewish patriarch Tevye in his song from "Fiddler on the Roof":

If I were a rich man . . . all day long I'd biddy biddy bum, if I were a wealthy man.

Tevye and his audience understand that he is expressing an improbable condition. Therefore, the subjunctive form *were* is used to reflect this. *Was* would indicate fact.

The committee recommends that new pension plans be established as soon as possible.

The committee wants these plans established, but the plans' existence is not yet factual.

Should she lose the election, she will have a very unhappy support staff.

You can see here that *verb auxiliaries* (helpers) like *should* and *would* also serve to express conditions and possibilities, as in

If I should ever become rich, I would be a great philanthropist.

VERBALS

What *looks* like a verb, *seems* to have the action of a verb, but lacks the horsepower to drive a sentence—and is actually a noun, adjective or adverb? It is the *verbal*, a pretender of sorts to the "action" throne.

It is important to recognize a verbal and understand its function to avoid writing incomplete sentences (see p. 46) or making errors in parallelism in a sentence (see p. 67). Verbals are classified as gerunds, participles or infinitives. We include them in this section as a preface to our discussion of nouns, adjectives and adverbs, as well as phrase construction, which is dealt with in Chapter 3. Let's briefly review the three verbals.

- Gerunds. These verbals, which always have an *-ing* form, are sometimes called *verb nouns* because they have the feel of some action even though they serve as the subject or object in a sentence:

  <u>Swimming</u> is a healthy, low-impact exercise.
  (Gerund, as subject)

  You can see that *swimming,* although seemingly an action word, is actually an activity, not an action. It cannot carry the requirements of a complete sentence. If you dropped the linking verb *is* from the previous sentence, you would have what is called a *sentence fragment,* in essence a phrase:

  Swimming, a healthy, low-impact exercise.

  Here's a pair of gerunds that serves as the object of a transitive verb:

  She really enjoys <u>swimming</u> and <u>weightlifting</u>.
  (Gerunds as the direct object)

Remember that gerunds are always nouns. They will act in the sentence the same way as nouns (see p. 24). Because the gerund also appears as the present tense of the verb with an *-ing* ending, it is sometimes confused with another verbal, the participle. We'll discuss that form now.

- Participles. These verbals, which have either an *-ing* or *-ed* ending, are always used as *adjectives* in a sentence. As an adjective (see p. 31), the participle generally will modify (give extra meaning to) a noun or a pronoun. Examples:

  <u>Hoisting</u> her protest sign high above her head, the 75-year-old demonstrator marched energetically toward city hall.

  Hoisting is part of the phrase that adds information about *demonstrator,* the subject of the sentence. The essential part of that sentence is the subject–verb combination, *demonstrator marched.*

<u>Hoisted</u> above the surf by the warm air, the intrepid flier guided her hang glider past the dangerous cliffs.

Hoisted describes the condition of the subject *flier*. As such, it makes this verbal (a participle) an adjective. As Chapter 3 will tell you, the introductory words in the previous sentence constitute a participial phrase. In Chapter 3, you'll see that using an introductory phrase that is too long keeps the reader from the key ingredients in any sentence—the subject and the verb. But we're getting ahead of ourselves.

- Infinitives. These are verbals that are formed by the use of *to* plus, in many cases, the present tense of a verb. Because of the use of *to* and the fact that they have no *-ing* forms, infinitives are easy to identify; however, their place as a part of speech (noun, adjective or adverb) is not always so easy to determine. Let's look at three examples:

The fiery coach needs <u>to win</u>.
(infinitive, as noun)

In this sentence, *to win* serves as the object of the transitive verb *needs*. The object *to win* answers the question *what*. As an object, it works as a noun in this sentence. The only verb in this sentence is *needs*.

"This is the way <u>to win</u>," the excited coach told his players.
(infin., as adj.)

The infinitive *to win* modifies (describes) the noun *way*. As page 29 tells you, a modifier of a noun is always an adjective. There are only two verbs in this sentence—*is* and *told*.

The embattled coach is eager <u>to win</u>.
(infin., as adv.)

In this sentence, the nature of the coach's eagerness is about winning—so the infinitive *to win* modifies the adjective *eager* (remember our discussion about the adjective that follows the linking verb and relates back to the noun?). In parts of speech, the adverb modifies an adjective (see p. 32).

These, then, are our three verbals. Remember that a verbal cannot sustain or drive a sentence; that is why they are not real verbs. (You can walk like a duck and talk like a duck, but that doesn't mean you're a duck!). Verbals can only be nouns, adjectives or adverbs.

This wraps up our examination of verbs. Recognizing a verb and using it well are keys to effective sentence construction. (Quick—how many verbs and verbals are in this paragraph?)

NOUNS

You'll recall (we hope) from elementary school that a *noun* can be a person, place or thing, and that it can appear in many parts of a sentence. For example, all of these words (and names) are nouns:

judge

Sara Jenkins

beach

influenza

intelligence

bravery

committee

You can see that these are not action words, but clearly, they can be the activators (or the receivers) of some action from a verb. Because nouns are such a common component of our sentences, they have many roles. We'll briefly list these components; however, you'll get a fuller explanation in Chapter 3, "The Sentence." Here they are:

1. As the subject of a sentence

   The <u>judge</u> reversed the lower court's decision.

   <u>Sara Jenkins</u> is a great newspaper editor.

   <u>Bravery</u> is an elusive trait in today's politics.

2. As the direct object of a transitive verb

   The governor named the <u>judge</u> to the blue-ribbon panel.

The Pulitzer committee selected <u>Sara Jenkins</u> to review the Panel's recommendations.

Sen. Smith cited <u>bravery</u> as the characteristic most needed in the coming century.

3. As the predicate nominative of a linking verb

   The winner of this year's Pulitzer Prize for commentary is <u>Sara Jenkins</u>.

   The trait cited most frequently by the committee was <u>bravery</u>.

4. As the object of a preposition

   Please send this letter to the <u>judge</u>.

   Your essay on <u>bravery</u> was thoughtful and compelling.

5. As a possessive or modifier

   The <u>judge's</u> nomination has been stalled by the committee.

We realize that some of this material has not yet been explained in the text and that much of it has a full discussion in several forthcoming chapters. Many of your questions about form and function of various parts of speech will soon be answered, especially in the next two chapters. You may also want to refer to Part II, "A Topical Guide to Grammar and Word Use," for some quick definitions and examples.

PRONOUNS

A *pronoun* "stands in" for a noun and sometimes is called a *noun substitute.* Pronouns add flexibility and variety to a sentence by keeping us from restating the same noun in that sentence.

However, pronouns can be more confusing in usage than nouns. Some of the most common grammatical problems relate to the use of pronouns in such areas as case (Chapter 5), antecedent agreement (Chapter 4), possessives (Chapter 5) and the selection of the proper pronoun to introduce a dependent clause (p. 28).

So, pay close attention as we review the different types of pronouns: personal, indefinite, relative and interrogative, and demonstrative.

PRONOUN TYPES

1. **Personal.** The most common pronoun type, the personal pronoun takes distinct forms in three cases: nominative (subjective), objective and possessive. Let's review them, from first-person singular to third-person plural:

Nominative	Objective	Possessive
I	me	my/mine
you	you	your/yours
he	him	his
she	her	her/hers
it	it	its
we	us	our/ours
you	you	your/yours
they	them	their/theirs

That's a substantial number of changes as you go through the possibilities of sentence configurations! You'll see the importance of proper selection of personal pronouns when you read the chapter on case. For example, when selecting the correct possessive pronoun, a writer is sometimes lured by the unnecessary but seductive apostrophe. The most common problem involves the *its/it's* decision; lest you think this is an easy distinction, you should wonder why errors in this choice are cropping up more frequently in daily newspaper headlines. Let's look at these two sentences:

The stock market registered <u>its</u> eighth straight gain of the month.
(personal possessive pron., modifies gain)

<u>It's</u> time for the stock market to return to normalcy.
(Combination of subject *it* and verb *is*—nothing is being modified.)

One reason for confusion about the use of apostrophes with pronouns as possessives is that the noun does use an apostrophe to form its possessive. So although *her's, your's* and *our's* are incorrect constructions, these noun possessives are correct with the apostrophe:

<u>Gingrich's</u> final term
(proper noun)

<u>stock market's</u> gain
(common noun)

Here's a sentence that will either completely illustrate this issue or will propel you to further confusion (we hope it's the former):

<u>It's</u> evident that the <u>stock market's</u> gain has a great deal to do with
(It is)   (possessive noun, needs apostrophe)

the <u>public's</u> perception of <u>its</u> connection to interest rates.
   (possessive noun)   (possessive pron., no apostrophe needed)

Got it? We hope so! If not, there are plenty of reinforcing lessons ahead.

2. Indefinite. Because pronouns such as *anyone, enough, many, most, none* and *several* reveal little if anything about their gender or number, they can cause troublesome subject–verb and antecedent *agreement* problems. (We'll discuss agreement in Chapter 4). For now, try to understand the *sense* of the sentence, so you can properly match subject, verb and *antecedent* (a word to which a pronoun refers).

The good news is that only a handful of indefinite pronouns can take either a singular or plural verb, depending on the sense of the sentence. They include:

all   most   none   some

<u>Most</u> of the coastal village <u>was</u> severely damaged by the storm.

<u>Most</u> of the passengers <u>were</u> rescued from the burning ship.

Some indefinite pronouns, such as *both, few, many* and *several,* are obviously plural.

<u>Many</u> <u>are</u> called, but <u>few</u> <u>are</u> chosen.

Indefinite pronouns such as *anybody* and *somebody* can be vexing when it comes to gender identification—and they can cause awkward writing. Which of the four choices below is correct? (See p. 171.)

<u>Anybody</u> can cast <u>his</u> ballot for town crier.

<u>Anybody</u> can cast <u>her</u> ballot for town crier.

<u>Anybody</u> can cast <u>his or her</u> ballot for town crier.

<u>Anybody</u> can cast <u>their</u> ballot for town crier.

3. Relative and interrogative. Pronouns such as *that, which* and *who* are easy to recognize, but they can be difficult to use properly. Examine the next four sentences and note the correct choices:

(Who/<u>Whom</u>) did the grand jury indict?

She is the type of leader (that/<u>who</u>) commands unwavering loyalty.

The aircraft carrier *Enterprise,* (that/<u>which</u>) is steaming now toward the Persian Gulf, is an intimidating spectacle.

This is one of those pens (<u>that</u>/which) (write/<u>writes</u>) upside down.

Using these pronouns correctly requires an understanding of case, antecedent agreement and restrictive and nonrestrictive clauses. Chapters 3, 4 and 5 deal with these topics. However, this is an appropriate place to mention a common error in relative pronoun use—the use of *that* to avoid a *who/whom* selection, as in

The police officers <u>that</u> stopped my car were polite but firm.
          (the correct pronoun is *who*)

The candidate <u>that</u> the voters selected has been indicted.
          (the correct pronoun is *whom*)

Who or *whom,* rather than *that,* must be selected when the antecedent (in these cases, *officers* and *candidate*) is human or when it takes on human qualities.

Be aware that the relative pronoun *who* has a separate possessive form (remember the problem of substituting subject–verb contractions for possessive pronouns, as in the *it's/its* issue?). The possessive of *who* is *whose*—not the subject–verb contraction *who's* (*who is*). Reflect on this sentence:

Alice Franklin, an 89-year-old widow <u>whose</u> Social Security
          (refers to Alice)

money was stolen this morning by neighborhood toughs, has found a hero <u>who's</u> determined to make city streets safer.
(*who is*)

4. Demonstrative. These pronouns are "pointers"—that is, they have a measure of specificity that leaves little room for doubt. They include *this, that, these* and *those.* They can stand alone as in:

<u>This</u> is exactly the kind of situation that will land you in court.
(refers to a specific instance)

Or they can modify other nouns (and become an adjective in the process):

<u>These</u> talk shows are driving me crazy!
(modifies *talk shows*)

ADJECTIVES

If a strong, direct verb lays a proper foundation for a sentence, then a creative and well-targeted *adjective* gives that sentence a special finish or luster that will set it apart.

Adjectives describe, limit and otherwise qualify nouns and pronouns. They do not modify verbs; that is the realm of the adverb. Adjectives are "picture words"; they enhance the detail of a sentence. They can also be overused and misapplied. Given their many nuances, adjectives challenge the writer to be on target with meanings.

TYPES OF ADJECTIVES

1. Descriptive. In creating a picture or adding detail to it, the adjective expands the meaning of a sentence and helps set a mood. Consider the differences in these two sentences (adjectives are underlined):

   Investors are questioning the <u>latest</u> proposal from the <u>new</u> Internet provider.

   <u>Skeptical</u> and <u>angry</u> investors are questioning the <u>latest</u> proposal from the <u>fledgling</u> Internet provider.

Which sentence tells you more and paints a fuller picture?

Careful writers use adjectives carefully. They are concerned more with content than with flashiness. For example, when the writer decided to give a stronger description of the Internet provider, she decided that *new* was bland and incomplete. She could have chosen from that storehouse known as the thesaurus such similar adjectives as:

youthful   latest   fresh   novel—or even neoteric (!)

However, *fledgling*—indicating an Internet provider that is untried, untested and definitely inexperienced—was the most accurate descriptor that the writer could employ.

2. Limiting. Whereas the descriptive adjective is colorful and artistic, the limiting adjective is more spartan. In blue jeans parlance, if the descriptive adjective is "designer label," the limiting adjective is "plain pockets." This adjective sets boundaries and qualifies (limits) meaning. Consider these examples:

The lost skiers had to hike <u>15</u> miles to reach help.
(The number *15* gives us a specific idea of just how far the skiers had to hike. Much can be inferred from this, although in this case, the writer did not choose to add more descriptive detail, such as *tortuous* or *snow-clogged miles.*)

"<u>This</u> turnover cost us the game," the coach said sadly.
(As you could see from the example on p. 29, *this* becomes an adjective when it modifies a noun, like *turnover*. Again, the adjective limits [focuses] the meaning of the sentence. The coach is referring to one specific *turnover*.)

Do you know <u>any</u> ways to improve your writing?
(Although the boundaries set here in specifying ways are very broad, *any* is seen as a limiting adjective because it provides no description or other helpful context. *Each* and *either* also fit into the category of limiting adjectives.)

DEGREES OF ADJECTIVES

Many adjectives and adverbs have three forms that show degree, intensity or comparison. For example, the trio of

high   higher   highest

moves from the *base* level (*high*) to a *comparative* level (*higher*), and then to the *superlative* level (*highest*). Obviously, at the superlative level, no higher comparison can be made.

Most affected adjectives take either the suffix *-er* or *-est* to show these changes in degree. However, some do retain their base form and merely add the adverbs *more* and *most* to show a change in degree, as in

controversial   <u>more</u> controversial   <u>most</u> controversial

You can see why the use of *more* with an adjective already converted to the comparative, such as *higher,* creates a funny-sounding (and ungrammatical) construction: *more higher.* See a further discussion of comparatives and superlatives in the section on adverbs.

THE PREDICATE ADJECTIVE

We hope you'll recall that an adjective can follow a linking verb (p. 17) and modify the subject of a sentence. In this form, it is called a *predicate adjective* because its relationship to the subject is transmitted through the verb—hence the idea of linking.

The company's advertising campaign is <u>offensive</u>.
(predicate adj.)
(*Offensive* is a predicate adjective. The verb *is* links the quality of being offensive to the noun *campaign*—hence, an *offensive campaign* [adjective modifying a noun].)

The fire marshal charged that the smoke detectors were <u>defective</u>.
(pred. adj.)
(Read this linking relationship as *defective detectors.*)

ADJECTIVES AS VERBALS

Two verbals, the participle and the infinitive (see pp. 22–23), can be classified as adjectives. Whereas the participle is *always* an adjective, the infinitive is only an adjective *when it modifies a noun.* (Infinitives can also act as a noun or as an adverb, depending on their role in a sentence.)

<u>Running</u> with a desperation that broadcast his fear, the pursesnatcher eluded his pursuers for only two blocks.
(*Running,* a participle, modifies the noun *purse-snatcher.* It acts as a descriptive adjective.)

The senator announced her decision <u>to vote</u> against the trade bill.
(The infinitive *to vote* modifies the noun *decision*; *to vote* characterizes or helps describe *decision*.)

ADVERBS

Like adjectives, *adverbs* also perform descriptive and limiting functions. Their uses in sentences, however, are far more complex. For example, an adverb can:

- modify a verb

  The suspect was driving <u>erratically</u> on the crowded freeway.
  (The adverb *erratically* describes or modifies the verb *was driving*; in this type of construction, an adverb often answers the question *how*.)

- modify an adjective

  He is <u>quite</u> handsome, don't you agree?
  (*Quite* modifies the adjective *handsome*; it states a degree of "handsomeness.")

- modify another adverb

  The rock star formerly known as Roadkill took his concert review <u>very</u> badly.
  (*Very* modifies the adverb *badly*, which together modifies the verb *took*; again, these adverbs answer the question *how*.)

- introduce a sentence

  <u>Why</u> do fools fall in love?
  (*Why* is an interrogative adverb; it modifies the verb *fall*.)

- connect two clauses

  The jury agreed that the plaintiff was defamed; <u>however</u>, it awarded only $1 in damages.
  (Because it links two clauses that could stand alone, *however* is called a *conjunctive adverb*.)

Many adverbs end in *-ly*, but don't always count on that for proper identification. Examine a sentence carefully to be sure—*slow* can be both adjective and adverb depending on how it is used in a sentence, but *slowly* can only be an adverb.

In addition to selecting the most appropriate and descriptive of adverbs for a sentence, writers should also be concerned about the proper positioning of an adverb. Although an adverb can be moved around to provide a change in emphasis, it's a good rule of thumb to position the adverb as closely as possible to the word it is supposed to modify. You don't want to confuse your intentions, which could have happened in the previous paragraph:

> Only slowly can be an adverb.

or

> Slowly can only be an adverb.
> (Surely the first sentence can't be correct—there are many other adverbs out there besides *slowly*.)

COMPARATIVES AND SUPERLATIVES

An adverbial *comparative* indicates a comparison between two units, and its *superlative* indicates the highest degree of quality between three or more units. Examples:

> Ohio's unemployment rate has risen faster than Indiana's.
> (*Comparative*—two states are being compared, through a modification of the verb *has risen*. Note the punctuation for *Indiana—unemployment rate* for that state is understood but not expressed.)

> Ohio's unemployment rate has risen the fastest of all Midwestern states.
> (*Superlative*—there is no higher degree of comparison available.)

Be sure that your meaning is clear when you employ a comparative or superlative:

> Hypertension is more pernicious than any chronic disease in the world today.
> (Besides being an amazingly sweeping statement, this sentence also implies that hypertension is also more pernicious than itself, because it, too, is a chronic disease. The last part of the sentence should read, *than any other chronic disease in the world today.*)

This is the <u>most</u> unique piece of art I have ever seen.
(Certain words, called *absolutes*, defy comparisons. *Unique*, an absolute, is already a superlative. So are *perfect, excellent, impossible, final* and *supreme*.)

It would suffice to say:

This is a <u>unique</u> piece of art.

PREPOSITIONS

Prepositions are the worker bees of sentence construction. They lead a quiet but important existence as they work with nouns and pronouns to create phrases and link these phrases to the rest of a sentence, as in

<u>of</u> the people, <u>by</u> the people, <u>for</u> the people

and

The courier arrived <u>with</u> the payroll.

Like many other parts of speech, prepositions can have tightly focused meanings. Writers sometimes make the wrong choices with such prepositional pairs as *among/between, beside/besides, beneath/ below, because of/due to* and *on/upon*. Part II of this book provides a brief discussion on the differences of these pairs.

The prepositions we most frequently use include:

at   by   for   from   in   of   on   to   with

Here is a brief list of the prepositions that are used less frequently (note that some are more than one word):

aboard	about	above	according to	across
after	against	ahead of	along	among
around	as far as	because of	before	behind
beside	besides	between	beyond	contrary to
despite	down	during	inside	into
like	near	next to	out of	over
past	per	since	through	throughout
toward	under	until	within	without

Prepositions link with nouns and pronouns to form *prepositional phrases,* as in *with the payroll,* in the beginning of this section. An important point of grammar here is the reminder that a pronoun must be in the objective case when it is the object of the preposition (nouns don't have an objective case change). So, it would *not* be correct to write (or say)

Between you and I, this marketing effort won't succeed.

The personal pronoun *I* changes to *me* in the objective case; the sentence should begin with

Between you and me . . .

The same is true for such phrases as

according to her   for us   to them

Indeed, prepositional phrases always have objects. The English poet John Donne understood this more than 300 years ago when he wrote

". . . never send to know for whom the bell tolls."

For more discussion of case, please see Chapter 5.

Besides (that's also a preposition) proper selection of case, writers should also be concerned about the excessive or unnecessary use of prepositions. Consider this bloated sentence (prepositional phrase underlined):

In reference to your term paper, I think that it is wordy and unfocused.

Using this prepositional phrase creates an unnecessary introduction and a resulting sentence that could be much more direct, as in

Your term paper is wordy and unfocused.

One final point about prepositions, long a part of grammatical lore: What is this business about *not* ending a sentence with a preposition (or perhaps we should say, with *with*)? If it was good enough for the writer of the hit song "Devil With a Blue Dress On," why can't you end with *with, to* or *on?* Well, we feel the same way about this as we do about cracking open fresh eggs with just one hand: Do it as long as you don't make a mess. Scrambling a sentence to move around a preposition can sometimes be awkward:

> This is a sentence <u>up</u> with which a good writer will not put.

You're looking for clarity, right? Isn't that what good writing is all *about?*

CONJUNCTIONS

Some cynics think that *conjunctions* are placed in a sentence to make it more complicated—that is, the sentence will become so long and bloated that it will need a conjunction to bridge it. They are correct about the linking function of a conjunction, but they are off the mark about what kind of sentence is created with it. In fact, a conjunction can be very helpful in maintaining rhythm and coherence, in addition to creating needed transitions of thought. Let's examine how they work in sentences.

COORDINATING AND SUBORDINATING CONJUNCTIONS

In its primary role, a conjunction coordinates (balances) clauses and phrases of equal weight. (For an in-depth discussion of clauses and phrases, see Chapter 3.) In linking two independent clauses, which could stand alone as two separate sentences, the coordinating conjunction links these clauses in one sentence because the writer decides to include them in a single, coordinated thought:

> The city council approved the zoning change, <u>but</u> it postponed a decision on the shopping center building permit.

A coordinating conjunction can also link simple words and phrases that are combined to show a relationship.

> He enjoys bungee-jumping <u>and</u> scuba diving.

> When in a difficult situation, be careful not to jump out of the frying pan <u>and</u> into the fire.

The most common *coordinating* conjunctions are:

and   but   for   nor   or   yet   while

When conjunctions are used to join clauses of unequal weight (that is, one clearly takes precedence and can stand by itself if necessary as a complete sentence), they are called *subordinating.* They often are used to introduce some material or to provide context or counterpoint to the main part of the sentence, as in

> <u>Unless</u> the negotiators can come to an agreement, the strike will begin at midnight.

> I will have to cancel the concert <u>unless</u> you can meet the fire marshal's exit requirements.

The most common subordinating conjunctions are:

after   although   as   as if   before   how   if
since   so   through   unless   while

Pay careful attention to use of the subordinating conjunction *as if.* Be wary of substitutes; a common error is the use of the preposition *like,* as in

> It looks <u>like</u> it will snow today.

Remember that prepositions cannot link a clause—only a phrase or single word. In the previous sentence, a writer has two choices to correct it:

> It looks <u>as if</u> it will snow today.

> It looks <u>like</u> snow today.

CORRELATIVE CONJUNCTIONS

These conjunctions, operating in pairs, are called correlative because they pair words, phrases and clauses to provide balance.

> Our vacation was <u>both</u> refreshing <u>and</u> exhausting.

<u>Neither</u> the players <u>nor</u> the coach has met with the media.
(Note—if the singular verb in this sentence seems odd, please see p. 61.)

The most common correlative conjunctions are:

both . . . and	either . . . or	neither . . . nor
not only . . . but also	whether . . . or	

ADVERBS THAT LOOK LIKE CONJUNCTIONS

Words like *accordingly, consequently, however, moreover, nevertheless* and *therefore* appear to have linking qualities; *however,* they are really adverbs that are inserted between two independent clauses to provide transition or a change in flow. For this reason, they are called *conjunctive adverbs.* (We hope this label doesn't add to your confusion.)

Our meeting lacks a quorum; <u>therefore,</u> we are adjourned until next Friday.
(See p. 106 about the use of a semicolon in this type of construction.)

INTERJECTIONS

If a preposition is a low-key part of speech, then the *interjection* is the wildly excitable member of this group. Also called the *exclamation,* it gives emotion and outburst to a sentence. It often stands alone and has its own punctuation, the *exclamation mark.*

Ouch!

Oh my!

<u>Whew</u>! A four-hour lecture on post-modernism is too much for me.

Note that a sentence may have a concluding exclamation mark while not including an interjection:

<u>Yippee</u>! We're so thankful this chapter is done!

CHAPTER 3

The Sentence

Sentences can be simple, compound, complex, compound-complex, incomplete, run-on, subordinated or oversubordinated. They can begin with prepositional phrases, present participle phrases, past participle phrases, gerund phrases, subordinate clauses, noun clauses, adjective clauses, adverb clauses, independent clauses or expletives.

Stop!

See how easy it is to get so wound up in the jargon of grammar that you begin to think writing is an esoteric act? See how easy it is to get confused, to get derailed, to forget that forming words into sentences is a basic human act we have all been performing for many, many years?

A sentence—from the Latin *sentire*, to feel—is a fundamental building block of thinking, speaking and writing. A sentence is words rubbing up against each other to spark ideas, to ignite emotions. A sentence is a logical pattern of words that most of us have been using since we were 18 months old.

"Give me that!" "I like this!" "Play with me!"

We *know* sentences. We say them silently to ourselves and out loud to our friends. We write them in letters and journals, in notes stuck on the refrigerator door. But when it comes to *studying* exactly how sentences are created, it's easy to feel so overwhelmed with definitions, exceptions, rules and regulations that we forget we are already experts. When we study the parts, types and pitfalls of sentences in this chapter, remember that we're doing so with a higher goal in mind: to write with clarity, precision and grace, to communicate fully.

When you see unfamiliar grammatical jargon, don't panic. Think of it as shorthand, a code that allows us to talk about how to create healthy, vibrant sentences. If we didn't use the code, if we had to say "a group of words that includes one independent clause and at least one dependent clause" every time we wanted to talk about a complex sentence, we'd be out of breath and out of patience fast. So bear with the code and learn it, keeping the goal in mind. Remember that when we investigate the sentence, we are investigating a familiar subject, an old friend.

On, then, to the sentence. A *sentence* is a self-contained grammatical unit that ends with a *full-stop* punctuation mark (period, question mark or exclamation point). It must contain a verb and a subject (stated or implied), and it must state a complete thought.

A sentence can be as concise as a single word: *Go. Stop. Wait.* (The subject *you* is implied.) It can be as expansive as one of William Faulkner's famous 100-plus word constructions. Regardless of length, grammatically correct sentences result from the same procedure: the selection, manipulation and coordination of sentence parts.

SENTENCE PARTS
PREDICATES AND SUBJECTS

A sentence can be divided into two parts: the *predicate* and the *subject*.

The *simple predicate* of a sentence is the verb. The *simple subject* is the noun or noun substitute.

	The	<u>dog</u>	<u>barked.</u>
		(simple	(simple
		subj.)	pred.)

The *complete predicate* includes the verb plus all its complements and modifiers. The *complete subject* includes the noun or noun substitute and all its complements and modifiers.

<u>The small dog</u>   <u>barked insistently.</u>
(complete subj.)   (complete pred.)

We can continue to describe and modify both the subject and the predicate parts of the sentence:

<u>The small, angry dog</u> <u>barked insistently, baring his teeth and snarling.</u>
(complete subj.)   (complete pred.)

In addition to modifiers and descriptive phrases, action verbs can be complemented by direct objects, indirect objects and prepositional phrases, all of which are considered part of the predicate. A *direct object* is any noun or noun substitute that answers the question *what* or *whom*. An *indirect object* tells *to whom* or *for what* that action is done. A *prepositional phrase* is a preposition followed by its object. These complements must be in the objective case. Recognizing them will help you avoid making errors in case. (These are your old friends from Chapter 2, "Parts of Speech.")

The dog attacked <u>the mail carrier</u>.
>(dir. obj.)

The dog attacked <u>her</u>.
>(dir. obj., objective case)

The mail carrier gave <u>the dog</u>   <u>a bone</u>.
>(indir. obj.)   (dir. obj.)

The dog snarled <u>at the children</u>.
>(prep. phrase)

The dog snarled at <u>them</u>.
>(obj. of prep., objective case)

The complement of a linking verb is a noun or adjective describing the subject. These words are also considered part of the predicate.

The dog was a <u>Chihuahua</u>.
>(pred. noun)

The mail carrier was <u>fearless</u>.
>(pred. adj.)

PHRASES AND CLAUSES

Phrases and clauses are the building blocks of sentences. A *phrase* is a group of related words that lacks both a subject and a predicate. Phrases come in two basic varieties: *prepositional phrases* (a preposition followed by its object) and *verbal phrases* (a form of the verb—infinitive, gerund or participle—that does not act as a verb, accompanied by its object or related material).

The dog is <u>behind a chain-link fence</u>.
>(prep. phrase)

The dog's goal is <u>to dig under the fence.</u>
(infin. phrase)

<u>Preventing the dog from digging under the fence</u> is the owner's goal.
(Gerund phrase, acting as a noun)

<u>Placing rocks along the fence line,</u> the owner tried to thwart the dog's efforts.
(Present participle phrase, acting as an adj. modifying *owner*.)

<u>Thwarted for only a day or two,</u> the dog managed to find a way under the fence.
(Past participle phrase, acting as an adj. modifying *dog*.)

Recognizing phrases and knowing what functions they perform can help you in at least two ways. First, you will not mistake a phrase, however lengthy or complex, for a sentence. Because a phrase does not include a subject (although it can certainly include a noun or pronoun) or a predicate, it cannot act as a sentence. What it is, as we will see later in this chapter, is a *fragment*. Second, you will not misplace a participle phrase because you recognize that it modifies a noun and must be placed as close as possible to that noun.

A *clause* is a group of related words that contains a subject and predicate. An *independent* or *main clause* is a complete sentence.

The owner gave up and bought a cat.

A *dependent* or *subordinate clause*, although it also contains a subject and predicate, does not express a complete thought. It is not a sentence and cannot stand alone.

After the Chihuahua dug under the fence for the third time
(dependent clause)

<u>After the Chihuahua dug under the fence for the third time</u>, the owner gave up and bought a cat.
(dep. clause linked with main clause)

Dependent clauses come in three varieties according to the function they perform in a sentence. A *noun clause* takes the place of a noun or a noun substitute; an *adjective clause* serves as an adjective; an *adverb clause* acts as an adverb.

<u>That the owner was still interested in having a pet</u>
(noun clause)
was a great surprise.
(*It,* a pronoun, can be substituted for the clause.)

The dog, <u>who had run away to the neighbors,</u> found a good home.
(adj. clause, modifies the noun *dog*)

<u>After the cat died,</u> the owner bought a parakeet.
(adv. clause, modifies the verb by answering *when*)

Recognizing dependent clauses is important. Not only will you avoid using them as sentences—the fragment error—but also you can learn to use these clauses to add variety to sentence structure.

TYPES OF SENTENCES

Sentences come in four varieties depending on the number and type of clauses they contain.

SIMPLE SENTENCES

A *simple sentence* contains one independent clause. The most common construction is subject–verb–object.

<u>Forecasters</u> <u>predicted</u> <u>flooding</u>.
(subj.)   (verb)   (obj.)

We can add modifiers—single words or phrases or a combination of both—but regardless of the number of words, the sentence remains simple if it contains a single clause.

National <u>forecasters</u> today <u>predicted</u> more <u>flooding</u> for the
(adj.)   (adv.)   (adj.)   (prep. phrase)
devastated delta region.

COMPOUND SENTENCES

A *compound sentence* has two or more independent clauses, each containing a subject and predicate and each expressing a complete thought. The two complete clauses, equal or nearly equal in importance, are linked (coordinated) by a conjunction and a comma, semicolon or colon. *And, but, or, nor* and *yet* are the conjunctions, sometimes referred to as *coordinating conjunctions.*

> <u>The region is suffering from severe flooding,</u> and <u>millions of acres</u>
> (indep. clause)   (conj.)(indep. clause)
>
> <u>will be affected.</u>
>
> The region is suffering from severe flooding; millions of acres will be affected.
> (clauses linked by semicolon)
>
> The region is suffering from severe flooding, and one thing is certain: Millions of acres will be affected.
> (three indep. clauses, linked by comma and conjunction, and colon)

Punctuation is probably the most common problem associated with compound sentences. Because the two (or more) clauses are independent—actually complete sentences on their own—they cannot be linked by a comma alone. The comma creates a brief pause that separates phrases or dependent clauses from the core of the sentence. By itself, it is too weak a punctuation mark to separate complete thoughts. A compound sentence needs both a comma and a coordinating conjunction. If you do not want to use a coordinating conjunction, use a semicolon or, occasionally, a colon. For more on punctuation, see "Run-on sentences" later in this chapter and Chapter 7, which focuses on punctuation.

COMPLEX SENTENCES

A *complex sentence* contains one independent (main) clause and at least one dependent (subordinate) clause. The subordinate clause depends on the main clause for both meaning and grammatical completion.

> <u>Because the region flooded,</u> <u>many Chihuahuas drowned.</u>
> (dep. clause)   (indep. clause)
>
> <u>The cats survived</u> <u>because they climbed trees.</u>
> (indep. clause)   (dep. clause)

In the two preceding complex sentences, conjunctions (*because*) introduce the dependent clauses. These words, sometimes called *subordinating conjunctions*, establish the relationship between the two sentence parts. Our language has a variety of such words, each with its own precise meaning. The careful writer chooses the subordinating conjunction that best expresses the specific relationship between the dependent and independent clauses. For example:

Relationship	Conjunctions
cause and effect	because, due to, as a result of, if
sequence	after, before, during, while
time, place	when, whenever, since, where, until, as long as

A dependent clause can also be subordinated to the main clause by relative pronouns (*who, whom, whose, which* or *that*). Note in the first of the following examples that the main clause can be interrupted by the dependent clause.

The parakeet <u>whose cage was opened</u> flew out of the house and
      (dep. clause)

up into a tree.

The cat was in the tree <u>that the parakeet chose</u>.
           (dep. clause)

COMPOUND-COMPLEX SENTENCES

A *compound-complex* sentence contains at least two main clauses and one dependent clause. The construction seems to invite wordiness, but a careful writer will refuse to fall into the trap. Here is a three-clause sentence that works:

<u>After the cat ate the parakeet,</u> <u>the owner was distraught,</u> <u>but she</u>
(dep. clause)   (indep. clause)

<u>remained an animal lover</u>.
(indep. clause)

If you find that a compound-complex sentence is out of control—so complicated that readers will lose the thread, so long that broadcasters will gasp for breath—break the sentence into two (or more) parts, being careful to maintain the relationship between subordinate and main thoughts.

A GOOD SENTENCE

You begin by choosing words carefully, respectful of their meanings and aware of their sounds and rhythms. You form the words into clusters and join the clusters with invisible seams. A pattern emerges.

You read it to yourself. It says precisely what you want it to say. It has grammatical unity. The idea is coherent; the statement, concise. You sit back to marvel.

Congratulations. You have written a good sentence.

SENTENCE ERRORS

Perhaps you haven't written a good sentence. Maybe you've fallen prey to one of the following ungrammatical or sluggish constructions: sentence fragment, run-on sentence, oversubordination or dead construction. Don't panic. You can catch this at the editing stage if you know what to look for.

SENTENCE FRAGMENTS

A fragment, literally an incomplete piece, is a group of words sheared off from or never attached to the sentence. The group of words may lack a subject, a predicate, a complete thought or any combination of the three. No matter what it lacks, it is not a grammatical sentence and should not stand alone. If you punctuate it as if it were a sentence, you have created a fragment.

Like this one.

Fragments can be single words, brief phrases or lengthy dependent clauses. The number of words is irrelevant. What matters is that the words do not meet the definition of a sentence. A common mistake is to look only for subject and verb and, having found them, to believe you have written a complete sentence. Remember, a sentence expresses a complete thought.

Although they were award-winning movie producers

contains a subject (*they*) and a verb (*were*) but does not express a complete thought. It is a dependent clause, a fragment.

They were award-winning movie producers.
(complete thought)

Although they were award-winning movie producers, their pictures made little money.
(complete thought)

Now that you know what a fragment is and what it must contain, avoiding or rewriting fragments should not be difficult. First, recognize that it is a fragment. It can be a single word, phrase or dependent clause. Now you have three choices: Rewrite the fragment to include all the parts it needs (subject, verb, complete thought); incorporate the fragment into a complete sentence; add to the fragment, making it a complete sentence. Here's how it works:

Their newest picture was a critical success. <u>But a commercial failure</u>.
(fragment)

Their newest picture was a critical success. <u>Unfortunately, it was also a</u> <u>commercial failure</u>.
(fragment rewritten as a complete thought)

Their newest picture, although a critical success, was a commercial failure.
(sentence rewritten to incorporate fragment)

Their newest picture was a critical success. <u>It was also a commercial failure that cost the studio $7.5 million.</u>
(addition to fragment forms a complete sentence)

Some accomplished writers will tell you that fragments serve a useful purpose. Advertising copywriters seem to have a particular penchant for fragments. In appropriate instances, to achieve particular effects, certain grammatical rules can be broken—and this is one of them. *Purposeful fragments*—consistent with the subject, the audience and the medium—are a matter of style. *Accidental fragments* are a grammatical error.

RUN-ON SENTENCES

A *run-on sentence* doesn't know when to quit. Rushing forward without proper punctuation, this construction may actually include two or three sentences. Length is not the issue here. A relatively short sentence, like the following one, can be a run-on.

The university announced a 20-percent tuition hike, students are calling for a daylong strike.

This sentence is actually two independent clauses run together with a comma. Using commas to link independent clauses (without the help of a conjunction) almost always results in a run-on sentence. In fact, this *comma-splice* error is the most common cause of run-on sentences. But if you can recognize an independent clause, and if you understand the limitations of the comma, you can avoid the error.

The most frequently used of all punctuation marks, the comma serves a variety of important purposes. But one job a comma rarely performs is creating a long pause between independent clauses. This function is performed by the semicolon, the period or, less commonly, the colon. When you force the comma to do a job for which it was not designed, you create a grammatically incorrect construction.

Rarely, and only with extreme care, a writer might violate the comma-splice rule. When a sentence is composed of two or more brief, parallel clauses, commas might be used.

Be correct, be concise, be coherent.

In certain kinds of writing—literary journalism or a stylish feature story, for example—a writer might purposefully create comma-splice run-ons to achieve a particular effect. But this kind of rule breaking depends on knowing and respecting the rule.

Comma-splice run-ons, in addition to being grammatically incorrect, almost always lack coherence. A comma signals readers that they are reading one continuous idea interrupted by a brief pause (the comma). Readers expect the words following a comma to augment or complement what they have just read. But in a comma-splice run-on, the sense of the sentence (actually two or more complete thoughts) denies the message of the comma. There is not one continuous idea. New thoughts are introduced without the benefit of connections between them (for example, *but, and, or*).

You can correct a run-on sentence in four ways:

1. Change the run-on sentence into two (or more) complete sentences by adding periods and capital letters.

The university announced a 20-percent tuition hike. Students are calling for a daylong strike.

2. If there is a close and equal relationship between the two (or more) complete thoughts (clauses) in the run-on, insert a semicolon between them to express this relationship. A semicolon shows this connection and allows the reader to move swiftly from the first sentence to the second. But semicolons are somewhat formal and a little stodgy. They may not work in all instances.

   The university announced a 20-percent tuition hike; students are calling for a daylong strike.

3. In a comma-splice run-on, connect the two sentences with a coordinating conjunction if the two parts are of equal weight. Use *and, but, or, nor, yet* or *so* according to the meaning of the sentence. Always use a comma before the conjunction.

   The university announced a 20-percent tuition hike, and students are calling for a daylong strike.

4. If the relationship between the two (or more) independent clauses is such that one clause depends on the other, rewrite the "dependent" sentence as a clause and place it in front of or following the main clause. Choose a subordinating conjunction that expresses the nature of the relationship and place it appropriately. Subordinating conjunctions include *after, because, while, when, where, since, if* and *although*.

   After the university announced a 20-percent tuition hike, students called for a daylong strike.

   Students are calling for a daylong strike because the university announced a 20-percent tuition hike.

OVERSUBORDINATED SENTENCES

Subordination, the fourth way just listed to correct a run-on sentence, is the technique of making one idea less important than, or subordinate to, another. Consider these sentences:

The Hager brothers co-wrote the summer hit "Bobzilla."

The Hager brothers have not talked to each other in three years.

Assuming the idea in the first sentence is the more important one, you can subordinate the idea in the second sentence by creating a dependent clause and attaching it to the main clause.

> Although the Hager brothers have not talked to each other in three years, they co-wrote the summer hit "Bobzilla."

> The Hager brothers, who have not talked to each other in three years, co-wrote the summer hit "Bobzilla."

Subordinating one idea to another is a useful sentence-building technique. But beware of oversubordination.

A string of dependent clauses or one excessively long dependent clause placed before the main sentence can slow the pace. You make your audience wait too long to get to the important idea, and you risk losing and confusing them.

> After not speaking to each other for three years following the legendary failure of their "Star Bob" trilogy, despite the efforts of family and friends to bring them together, the Hager brothers co-wrote the summer hit "Bobzilla."
> (Oversubordination)

There are too many ideas here for one sentence. The two subordinate clauses that precede the main idea bog down the sentence and slow the reader's comprehension. The sentence needs to be rewritten, shortening and combining the introductory ideas or giving them a sentence of their own.

> <u>After not speaking to each other for three years following the legendary failure of their "Star Bob" trilogy which, although it starred Bruce Willis and had the biggest advertising budget ever allotted to a movie in the history of movie making, was a commercial failure,</u> the Hager brothers co-wrote the summer hit "Bobzilla."
> (lengthy introductory clause underlined)

This sentence is sagging under the weight of a 45-word introductory clause that takes the reader in so many directions that the idea of the main clause is lost. To solve the problem, the introductory clause can be shortened or it can become a sentence (or two) of its own.

Another kind of oversubordination occurs when several dependent clauses are tacked onto the end of the main clause. The result is a confusing succession of modifiers.

> The Hager brothers, who have not talked to each other in three years, co-wrote the summer hit "Bobzilla," which was filmed on location in Jersey City, N.J., after negotiations with the city of Newark broke down following a dispute between the production crew and local sanitation workers who were on strike.

This sentence seems never to end, with a parade of phrases and clauses following the main idea. All these ideas confuse the reader and dilute meaning. Once again, there is too much here for a single sentence. The solution is to rewrite it as several sentences.

Sentences can also suffer from oversubordination when a main clause is sandwiched between two dependent clauses. The result is often an awkward-sounding (or awkward-reading), choppy sentence.

> Although the Hager brothers have not talked to each other in three years, they co-wrote the summer hit "Bobzilla," which brought them international acclaim but only served to exacerbate their sibling rivalry.
>
> (front and back subordination)

In this sentence, it would help to shorten the phrase *which brought them international acclaim* to *internationally acclaimed* and use it to modify Bobzilla. But you are still stuck with an awkward, tacked-on-sounding final phrase. Two sentences would be best.

DEAD CONSTRUCTIONS

Perhaps they are holdovers from term paper writing style, but these constructions have little place in good writing: *it is* and *there is*. In most cases, these words, called *expletives*, merely take up space, performing no function in the sentence. They not only add clutter but also often rob the sentence of its power by shifting emphasis from what could be a strong verb to a weaker construction—a linking verb (*is, was* and other forms of *to be*).

> <u>There was</u> a <u>protest</u> by angry animal-lovers in front of
> (verb potential)
>
> International House of Pets today.
>
> Angry animal-lovers <u>protested</u> in front of International House of Pets today.　　(stronger verb)
>
> <u>It is</u> their <u>intent</u> to halt "business as usual."
> (verb potential)

They <u>intend</u> to speak "business as usual."
(stronger verb)

In addition to strengthening the sentence by using an action verb, avoiding *there is/there are* constructions has another benefit: simpler subject–verb agreement. *There* is not usually a subject. Whether you use *is* or *are* depends on what follows the verb.

There <u>is</u> a <u>law</u> prohibiting the sale of endangered-species animals.

There <u>are</u> <u>plans</u> to enforce it.

Looking for the subject after the verb often creates agreement confusion. Avoid both the confusion and the dead construction by restructuring the sentences. For example:

The sale of endangered-species animals is illegal.

The city plans to enforce the law.

It is/there is constructions are not entirely without value. You might purposefully choose this structure to emphasize the subject and change the meter of the sentence.

It was the mayor who cast the deciding vote against the ordinance.
(emphasis)

The mayor cast the deciding vote against the ordinance.
(no emphasis)

A good rule to follow is this: If *it is/there is* merely takes up space in the sentence, restructure the sentence. Rescue the "hidden verb" and avoid agreement problems. If on occasion you want to emphasize the subject, use *it is/there is,* but use it sparingly.

THE LEAD SENTENCE

The first sentence is important to all writers, whether they are beginning an essay, a novel or a cookbook. But for media writers, the first sentence takes on added dimension. Competing for a reader's, viewer's or listener's time and attention, you must start off strong—whether you write traditional news stories, feature material, press releases, advertising copy or any other form of public communication.

In a traditional news story or press release, be it for print or broadcast, the first sentence is designed to give the audience a concise, comprehensive summary of the most important elements of the story. Although other forms of media writing like feature stories (print or broadcast) and advertising copywriting do not require this summary lead approach, they too demand that the writer has a clear sense of what is new or interesting about the material. This ability to recognize the essence of the material is central to being able to write a strong lead. Combining this ability (learned, with time and practice, with reading and writing) with your language skills will help you craft the important lead sentence.

You must be cautious, for the summary lead approach, with its admonishments to tell everything (who? what? when? where? how?) in one sentence, can open the door to bad writing. Packing a sentence with all this material increases the chance that you write a muddled, rambling or otherwise awkward sentence. Run-ons and oversubordination are common problems because you have so much information to include.

> State lawmakers failed to resolve a budget-balancing stalemate, they worked all week but had to recess for the weekend late Friday night.
> (run-on)

> After failing to resolve a budget-balancing stalemate, even though they worked all week, state lawmakers recessed for the weekend late Friday night.
> (oversubordination)

> After failing all week to resolve the budget-balancing stalemate, state lawmakers recessed for the weekend late Friday night.
> (improved)

Writing a simple lead sentence with subject–verb–object construction is sometimes difficult because of the amount of information you must include. Do remember that compound and complex sentences, if constructed economically, can be both clear and concise.

> Food prices rose 2 percent, but the cost of transportation remained the same, according to figures released yesterday by the federal government.
> (compound lead sentence)

The local school board voted last night to allow the distribution of birth control information in district high schools after health officials presented disturbing new data on teenage pregnancy. (complex lead sentence)

In non-news writing, the lead sentence is often meant to grab attention and pull the reader or listener into the message. Crisp, dynamic sentences are the key, as in this simple but powerful two-sentence feature lead for a story on Atlantic City land speculation:

The most important game in this town is not craps, or blackjack, or roulette. It is real estate, and nobody plays it better than Resorts International.

Consider this attention-grabbing lead that introduces an eight-page advertising insert for the famous M.D. Anderson Cancer Center at the University of Texas:

Everything causes cancer.

Of course, all sentences should be constructed grammatically, powerfully and gracefully. The lead, however, deserves your special attention.

CHAPTER 4

Agreement—Rules, Exceptions and Common Sense

Let's face it: Rules are rules—and there are a lot of them when it comes to agreement.

Despite that, we automatically make "proper" decisions about such things as subject-verb agreement in our informal, often rapid-fire speech. Even with his suspicious educational pedigree, the Bluto-bashing comic hero Popeye never would have committed this grammatical gaffe:

"I are what I are."

Similarly, none of us would say, "**I are** a writer" or "**she am** an editor."

Why wouldn't we? It is because our eyes and ears are "tuned" to realize that "it just doesn't seem right," mainly through years of reading and listening. Naturally, it is easier for us to detect when one part of speech (the singular pronoun *I*) clashes with another (the plural verb *are*) in a short, simple construction. It's akin to following a simple direction of "snapping part A into part B" when the letters are clearly marked—and when you have only two parts to assemble. This is easy enough to understand. So what's wrong with this much longer sentence?

One of the deadliest forest fires in California history have destroyed three communities near the Nevada border.

The problem is that the singular subject (*one*) does not agree with the plural verb (*have*). Losing track of the true subject will lead to an improper choice of verb number. As you will recall from Chapter 2, the object of a preposition—in this case, *fires*—cannot be the subject of the sentence. This sentence has proper agreement:

> One of the deadliest forest fires in California history <u>has destroyed</u> three communities near the Nevada border.
> (Note that one way not to be confused by the prepositional phrase is to read the subject as *one fire . . . has.*)

Like many aspects of our grammar, the function of agreement is not always clear and straightforward. You can see it in this sentence, which could be a watchword for decisions on agreement:

> A <u>number</u> of rules <u>are</u> easy to follow, and <u>none</u> <u>is</u> without logic.
> (subj.)   (verb)   (subj.) (verb)

An important function of grammar is to instill order in writing. The purpose of such order is to facilitate creativity and rhythm, not to stifle them. There are times, however, when rigid adherence to a rule results in awkwardness. In these cases, consider rewriting. For example, the following sentence is grammatically incorrect, although its usage is fairly common in everyday speech:

> <u>Everyone</u> has a right to <u>their</u> opinion.

The slavishly rigid grammarian, recognizing that a singular subject cannot be linked to a plural pronoun, might opt for a correct but awkward-sounding alternative:

> <u>Everyone</u> has a right to <u>his or her</u> opinion.

It's correct but thick, and lacking in rhythm. A simple rewrite solves the problem, is grammatically correct and sounds smooth:

> <u>People</u> have a right to <u>their</u> opinions.

So—let's pair correctness with harmony as we explore these areas of agreement:

- subject–verb
- pronoun reference
- tense agreement
- parallelism

SUBJECT–VERB AGREEMENT

Consider this seemingly straightforward rule:

A verb must agree with its subject in number.

Following this rule actually involves two steps:

1. identifying the real (or true) subject
2. deciding whether that subject is singular or plural

The first step is relatively easy—but the second has tripped up even the most seasoned writers. From your earlier reading you know what a subject is *not*.

- It is *not* the object of a preposition.

  <u>Between</u> these two extremes <u>lies</u> the real <u>solution</u>.
          (obj. of prep.) (verb)   (subj.)
  (*Solution* is the real subject. *Extremes,* the object of the preposition *between,* is plural; although it is physically close to the verb, it has no effect on the verb's number. So, you can read this sentence as *The real solution lies between these two extremes.*)

- It is *not* the object of a gerund.

  <u>Creating</u> new employment opportunities <u>is</u> her top priority.
  (subj. [ger.])   (verb)
  (*Creating,* a gerund, is the real subject. [Remember our discussion on p. 22?] *Opportunities,* the gerund's object, cannot influence the verb's number.)

- It is *not* a phrase that is parenthetical to the true subject.

  The welfare <u>appropriation, as well as several pro-environment</u>
          (subj.)   (parenthetical phrase)
  <u>resolutions, was sent</u> to the subcommittee for hearings.
         (verb)
  (Phrases such as *along with* and *as well as* merely modify the real subject of a sentence. They do not turn that subject into compound, or plural, construction.)

- It is *not* the expletive *there* or *here.*

<u>There</u> <u>have been</u> many <u>cases</u> of influenza <u>reported</u> this week.
(explet.) (verb)   (subj.)   (part of verb)
(Arguably, this sentence could be much more on point, as in *Many cases of influenza have been reported this week.* This is just an example to help you "get in shape" for finding the true subject.)

To recap this discussion of false subjects, here is a list of correct subject–verb combinations; both sentence parts are underlined:

The <u>rate</u> of farm failures <u>is dropping</u>.
   (subj.)   (verb)

<u>Creating</u> prize-winning commercials <u>was</u> Dan's lifelong dream.
(subj.)   (verb)

The <u>fitness center</u>, along with the espresso and wine bars,
   (subj.)
<u>was destroyed</u> in the fire.
(verb)

<u>Here</u> <u>are</u> the <u>announcements</u> on the president's agenda.
(explet.)(verb)(subj.)

Now that we have focused on what a subject *is not,* let's be more direct and examine just what a subject *is.* You will recall from the discussion of sentences in Chapter 3 that the subject is often the starting point of a sentence. Most often it is a noun or a pronoun, and it generally is a person, place or thing. It generally appears before the verb, and although it may follow the verb in certain constructions, it is directly connected to the verb in creating action or in being acted on.

Identifying whether the subject of a sentence is singular or plural sometimes requires some analysis. Let's examine this area in three ways:

- when the subject is always singular
- when it is always plural
- when it could be both

THE ALWAYS-SINGULAR SUBJECT

This area features several firm rules that should give you little trouble:

When used as a subject, the pronouns *each, either, anyone, everyone, much, no one, nothing* and *someone* always take singular verbs.

Everyone has been seated.

Much has been said about her performance.

Each of the wines has its special personality.

When *each, either, every* or *neither* is used as an adjective, the noun it modifies always takes a singular verb.

Every jar of pickles was spoiled.

Neither choice seems very attractive.

The personal pronoun *it,* when used as the subject of a sentence, always takes a singular verb.

As President Harding said, it wasn't his enemies who brought him down; it was his friends.

When *the number* is used as the subject of a sentence, it always takes a singular verb, no matter what the number of the noun in the prepositional phrase.

The number of Rollerblading injuries has dropped dramatically.

Note that the article *the* is more definite than the article *a. The number* implies an organized unit. *A number* refers to an undefined amount; we don't know how many, but we do know it is more than one. Therefore, this sentence would be correct:

A number of deranged stockbrockers were storming the
(subj.)   (verb)
headquarters of the U.S. Federal Reserve.

Subjects that stand for definable units of money, measurement, time, organization, food and medical problems always take singular verbs.

Five thousand dollars is the minimum bid for the foreclosed property.

<u>Twenty-six miles, 385 yards is</u> the traditional distance for the marathon.

<u>Six hours of swimming has</u> turned him into a giant prune.

<u>The United Auto Workers is</u> standing firm on its contract demands.

<u>Rice and beans is</u> an unusual breakfast dish.

<u>Measles wears</u> down parents as well as children.

Plural words that require singular verbs can sound awkward. For example, if you thought that the first of the preceding sentences sounded strained, you could easily rewrite it to eliminate any conflict:

<u>The city has set</u> $5,000 as the minimum bid for the foreclosed property.

A singular subject followed by such phrases as *together with* and *as well as* always takes a singular verb because those phrases are merely a modification of their subjects.

The new <u>Internet service company,</u> as well as two of its proposed new business plans, <u>has</u> attracted the attention of venture capitalists.
(In truth, many *together with* and *as well as* constructions can be awkward. There could be more direct ways to say the same thing.)

When all parts of a compound subject are singular and refer to the same person or thing, the verb is always singular.

The <u>president</u> and <u>board chairman</u> <u>is</u> Tom Henderson.
   (subj.)   (subj.)   (verb)

THE ALWAYS-PLURAL SUBJECT

When a compound subject is joined by the conjunction *and*, it always takes a plural verb if the subjects refer to different persons or things and if the subject cannot be considered a unit.

<u>Two partridges</u> and <u>one pear tree</u> <u>were discovered</u> on the twelfth day of the archeological dig.

(Note that although the part of the compound subject closer to the verb is singular, the entire subject still takes a plural verb. The rule is different for *or, neither. . . nor* and *either. . . or* constructions, as you will see in the next part of this section.)

When acting as the subject of a sentence, indefinite pronouns such as *both, few, many* and *several* always take plural verbs.

<u>Many</u> <u>are</u> cold, but <u>few</u> <u>are</u> frozen.

Well-recognized foreign plurals require plural verbs if they do not denote a unit.

The news <u>media</u> <u>are</u> under attack for <u>their</u> coverage of the "Bingo-gate" scandal.

(The singular of the Latin plural *media* is *medium*. Note also the use of the plural possessive pronoun *their* to provide consistency in antecedent selection.)

Her upper vertebrae were crushed in the accident.

(The singular of the Latin-derived *vertebrae* is *vertebra*.)

A number as the subject takes a plural verb because it does not denote a cohesive unit.

<u>A number</u> of ambitious politicians <u>have arrived</u> at the convention.
(subj.)   (verb)

THE SINGULAR OR PLURAL SUBJECT

Our language contains a series of agreement exceptions that may seem a bit maddening until they are examined carefully.

When a compound subject contains the conjunction *or* or *but* or contains an *either. . . or* or *neither. . . nor* correlative, the subject closer to the verb determines the number of the verb.

The bank <u>stocks</u> or the municipal <u>bond has</u> to be sold.
(plural subj.) (sing. subj.) (sing. verb)

Neither <u>he</u> nor his <u>associates</u> <u>have admitted</u> any blame.
(sing. subj.) (plural subj.) (plural verb)

If you must use a correlative conjunction, consider placing a plural subject closer to the verb. Changing the preceding sentence to "Neither his associates nor he has . . ." may be correct, but it sounds awkward.

Depending on their meaning in each particular sentence, collective nouns and certain words that are plural in form may take a singular or plural verb. Once again, the test of a unit can be applied. If a word indicates that persons or things are working together as an identifiable unit, it takes a singular verb.

Here are some examples of the proper use of the singular verb. We'll follow each example with a plural use when appropriate.

Politics <u>is</u> a topic to avoid at parties.

But note: The mayor's <u>politics</u> <u>are</u> offensive.
(*Practiced political principles* is the meaning here, not the concept of *politics*. If you think of this politician as spreading offensive political practices, the meaning becomes more clear.)

Acoustics <u>is</u> the scientific study of sound.

But note: The <u>acoustics</u> in this auditorium <u>are</u> deteriorating.

The jury <u>looks</u> concerned.

But note: The jury <u>were polled</u> on the split verdict.
(Because the jurors weren't unanimous in their findings, they now are being considered individually.)

If you are convinced that a plural verb is required with a collective noun, but it just doesn't look right to you, consider a rewrite, such as

The <u>jurors</u> <u>were polled</u> on their split verdict.

Pronouns such as *any, none* or *some* and nouns such as *all* and *most* take singular verbs if they refer to a unit or a general quantity. They take plural verbs if they refer to amount or individuals.

All of the retirement complex was destroyed.
(general)

All of the negotiable bonds are missing.
(amount)

Most of the day's work was wasted.
(general)

Most of the team members were uninjured.
(amount)

None of the prosecution witnesses is expected to testify today.
(In this sense, *none* means *no one witness.*)

None of the stolen goods were recovered.
(number)
(The sentence cannot mean that no one good was recovered; it means that
no goods were recovered.)

None is a particularly maddening pronoun, and its use causes a
great deal of debate. We believe that the word *none* (*no one*) is almost
always singular. However, in the following sentence, a writer's selection of plural predicate nominative (*women*) makes the intended
number of *none* clear:

None of the indicted stockbrokers are women.

Still, we challenge you to find more than a handful of examples in
which *none* would have to be used in the plural sense for greater clarity. Here's one:

None of these pants fit.
(In this construction you'd be hard-pressed to read *not one pant fits*. Sorry
about the pun. . . .)

When a subject is a fraction, or when it is a word such as *half,
part, plenty* and *rest*, its intended number is suggested by the
object of the preposition that follows it.

Three-fourths of Iowa farmland is under water this morning.
(subj.)   (obj. of prep.)   (verb)

Three-fourths of payroll checks have been lost.
(subj.)   (obj. of prep.)   (verb)

<u>Half</u> of the <u>rent money</u> <u>is</u> missing.
(subj.)   (obj. of prep.) (verb)

<u>Half</u> of the <u>rent receipts</u> <u>are</u> missing.
(subj.)   (obj. of prep.) (verb)

PRONOUN REFERENCE: LOOKING FOR AGREEABLE ANTECEDENTS

As noun substitutes, pronouns offer a certain economy to sentences. However, they can also cause irritation because of their unfortunate ability to confuse the meaning of a sentence. Because a pronoun requires an antecedent (a noun to which the pronoun refers), its link to the antecedent is important for sentence clarity.

As an example, what's your guess as to the *she* in the following sentence?

When the officer spotted the robbery suspect in the parking garage, <u>she</u> quickly ducked behind a moving van.

To employ the classic line of actor Clint Eastwood, "Are you feeling lucky today? Are you?" In the preceding example, you've got a 50-50 chance of making the correct choice—did the officer or the suspect duck behind the van?

Without a clear connection between pronoun and antecedent, the focus of a sentence softens. If your readers search in vain for a clear reference for the pronoun, you have engaged in a false economy. It's time to rewrite, as in

Spotting the robbery suspect in the parking garage, the officer quickly ducked behind a moving van.

A more difficult problem with pronouns is *number and person agreement* with antecedents. Consider these sentences:

Jughead is one of the funniest <u>graduate students</u> <u>who</u>
                              (antecedent)   (pron.)
<u>have</u> ever <u>attended </u>this university.
(verb)
(Many graduate students figure in this assessment. Jughead is *among* the funniest; he does not stand alone. The writer is referring to a number of

funny students who have attended the university; hence the plural verb is correct. Objects of prepositions can be antecedents; those objects are most often nouns, and a pronoun can substitute for them.)

Heavenly Norway is the <u>only brand</u> of sardines <u>that</u> <u>is packed</u> in
                           (antec.)   (pron.)(verb)
single-malt Scotch whiskey.

(Obviously, there are many brands of sardines. As asserted by the writer, however, only one is packed in whiskey. The relative pronoun *that* substitutes for the singular noun *brand*.)

The sales manager's <u>presentation</u> was flashy, but not many
                             (antec.)
buyers were swayed by <u>it</u>.
                       (pron.)

(You should not be fooled by the possessive *manager's*. Obviously, it modified *presentation*.)

<u>Neither</u> of the men had <u>his</u> sentence reduced.
(Subj.)   (pron.)

(As you recall, *neither* takes a singular verb. It follows that a possessive pronoun (*his*) referring to *neither* would stay in the same number.)

Remember: A pronoun agrees with its antecedent in both number and person. Stay consistent, and make your references clear.

TENSE AGREEMENT: KEEPING TIME IN STEP

It's unreasonable to think that you cannot shift verb tenses in the same sentence or paragraph. In fact, you may need to change tenses to show correct sequence and historical context:

Although she <u>was</u> a reserve guard last year, Elizabeth now
                 (past tense)
"<u>rides</u> the bench" only after her deadly three-pointers <u>have given</u>
(present tense)   (pres. perfect tense)
her team a comfortable edge.

This is a correct tense sequence. The two shifts make sense because they permit us to understand a chronology. Words such as *although* and *after* help us shift tense smoothly. However, that smooth flow does not exist in the following sentence:

> Frankie <u>is</u> a procrastinator, but no amount of guilt-ridden scolding
> (pres. tense)
> <u>was</u> going to change him.
> (past tense)

This is a confusing shift. The "time-warping" verbs cause the reader to lose perspective.

Note that in journalistic style, much reporting is done in the past tense. For the sake of immediacy, however, many headlines are written in the present tense. This is sometimes referred to as the *historical present.*

> Headline: President <u>Threatens</u> Veto of Tax Bill
>
> WASHINGTON—The president <u>said</u> today that he will veto a Senate bill that calls for an immediate 15 percent decrease in both personal and corporate income taxes.

Many news writers use the historical present to create an effect of immediacy or to show that an event, statement or condition is ongoing. The present tense often appears in the lead paragraph, and then the writer shifts into the past tense as the story continues:

> WASHINGTON—The president <u>says</u> he will not be moved.
>
> At a press conference today in the Rose Garden, he <u>threatened</u> to veto a Senate bill that would immediately cut personal and corporate income taxes by 15 percent.

Direct quotes don't always work well with the historical present. Even though the tense of the quotation should be preserved, its report should not. This would look odd:

> "I will not be moved," the president <u>says</u>.

In this case it would be better to make consistent use of the past tense:

> "I will not be moved," the president <u>said</u>. "I will fight for a responsible and balanced budget," he <u>promised</u>.

Another example of the historical present typically occurs in accident stories. The change in tense in the second paragraph is correct and logical:

> One woman <u>was killed</u> and three others <u>were injured</u> Tuesday night when their sports car <u>skidded</u> on icy roads on U.S. Highway 20 at Santiam Pass and <u>collided</u> with a log truck.
>
> Dead <u>is</u> Sarah Jane Ridgeway, 28, of Creswell.

Remember that tense agreement is an attempt to preserve historical sequence and context. Look for abrupt and illogical changes of tense. Above all, be consistent.

PARALLEL STRUCTURE

Some problems of tense agreement indicate another writing problem—defects in *parallel structure*. A sentence is considered parallel when its various units are in relative balance. When a sentence lacks parallelism, its focus softens and its rhythm falters.

COMMON ERRORS IN PARALLELISM

1. Mixing diverse or clashing elements in a phrase or series.

   > She enjoys <u>books, movies</u> and "<u>surfing</u>" the Internet.

   Why is this sentence unbalanced? It contains three nouns in a series, but the third noun is a verbal (gerund). It throws off the meter; it lacks parallel structure. This sentence could easily regain its rhythm:

   > She enjoys <u>reading books, watching movies</u> and "<u>surfing</u>" the <u>Internet.</u>

   In the next problem sentence, an adjective clashes with a noun:

   > Our economic recovery plan is <u>comprehensive</u>
   >   　　　　　　　　　　　　　　　　　(adj.)
   > and a brilliant <u>innovation</u>.
   >   　　　　　　　(noun)

Using two adjectives to complement the linking verb makes it parallel:

Our economic recovery plan is <u>comprehensive</u> and <u>innovative</u>.

Another problem in series construction involves a compound direct object that is broken off by a dependent clause. Such a break startles and confuses the reader:

The stock analyst discussed the mutual funds <u>market,</u> interest rate <u>forecasts,</u> and <u>that tax loopholes were becoming difficult to find</u>.

As this series develops, the reader expects to read a short series of objects following the verb discussed, such as:

. . . the mutual fund <u>market,</u> interest <u>rates</u> and the <u>scarcity</u> of tax loopholes.

This solution provides a "clean" series of three nouns as part of the direct object, making the sentence briefer and more direct.

2. Mixing verbals.

This is another example of selectively <u>using favorable statistics</u>
(ger. phrase)
and then to <u>write a report</u> around that biased selection.
(infin. phrase)

Here a gerund and an infinitive conflict. The sentence would be parallel if only gerunds were used:

. . . of selectively <u>using</u> favorable statistics and <u>writing</u> a report around that biased selection.

Here is another example of improperly mixing verbals:

Kathleen is a competitor who enjoys <u>seeking</u> challenges and
(ger.)
<u>to rise</u> to the top of her profession.
(infin.)

Why not use two verbs and be more direct?

Kathleen is a competitor who <u>enjoys</u> challenges and <u>wants</u> her profession's highest achievements.

3. Unnecessarily changing voice.

Verbs can have active or passive voices (see Chapter 6). Writers choose a voice according to the need to have the subject perform the action or to have it acted on. Generally, it is best to be consistent in voice. Shifting voice can disrupt the flow of a construction, as in this example:

The burglars <u>took</u> all the silver and china, but the jewelry and
      (active)
guns <u>were left</u> undisturbed.
    (passive)

It is much simpler to stay with one subject and write:

The <u>burglars</u> <u>took</u> all the silver and china but <u>left</u> the jewelry and guns.
  (subj.)   (active)   (active)

4. Unnecessarily changing subjects.

<u>One</u> never should argue with a referee; <u>people</u> should know that by now.

Besides creating a stilted construction with both singular and plural subjects, the writer also is wasting words. The sentence would read better this way:

<u>People</u> should know by now that <u>they</u> shouldn't argue with a referee.

SEXISM AS PART OF PARALLEL STRUCTURE

Although sexism may seem to be a cultural and ethical issue rather than a grammatical one, the equal treatment of the sexes is another way to ensure parallelism in your writing. Sexism and other *-isms* are discussed in depth in Chapter 10; however, for purposes of this chapter, we ask you to consider these examples of sexism in writing and note the inconsistencies in their logic and content:

1. The use of the generic *he* when referring to a noun of unknown gender.

   A small-town <u>mayor</u> often is in the best position to judge the civic commitment in <u>his</u> community.

2. Presumed maleness of certain nouns representing a position or class, even if it appears ludicrous.

   <u>Elizabeth</u> is an outstanding <u>spokesman</u> for her organization.

3. Demeaning or unequal treatment of the sexes.

   Debating tonight are the leading senatorial candidates: <u>Wall Street lawyer</u> Harold Smythe and Amanda Johnson, a <u>pert, blue-eyed grandmother of three</u>.

   The men's basketball team posted its 10th straight win, while the ladies' team <u>hung their ponytails in defeat</u>.

4. The use of courtesy titles (*Miss, Mrs., Ms.*) for women as an indication of marital status when the only courtesy title available for men (*Mr.*) reflects no such status.

Parallel structure is one of the main building blocks of sentence coherence. Proper use of it does not mean that your writing is rigid. Instead of being too restrictive, parallel structure can give great power and creativity to your work. It can make your writing orderly and easily understood.

All writing for mass communication demands clarity and honesty. Achieving grammatical agreement—whether it is the correct matching of the subject and the verb number or the equal treatment of gender—will give your writing the ring of truth and coherent order.

CHAPTER 5

Case

Nouns and pronouns take several forms, or *cases,* to indicate their function in a sentence. In the English language, we are fortunate to be dealing with only three cases: the nominative (subjective), objective and possessive. Other languages will call on you to also master the ablative and dative (don't ask), so consider yourself lucky!

Case requires changes to a noun only in its possessive form and to pronouns in all three of their forms.

Here are some examples of how we use case to show different functions:

- initiation of action (nominative)

  She refuses to settle the lawsuit.
  (Personal pronoun *she,* as subject of sentence, is in nominative case.)

- reception of action (objective)

  The judge asked her to reconsider.
  (Personal pronoun *her,* as indirect object, is in objective case.)

- indication of possession (modification)

  His new movie is drawing rave reviews.
  (Personal pronoun *his,* modifying the subject *movie,* is in possessive case.)

  The president's ratings continue to improve.
  (Noun *president's,* modifying subject *ratings,* is in possessive case.)

It's not that complicated, right?

Actually only nine pronouns have some change in case, and all nouns change only in their possessive form. The change to nouns requires the use of an apostrophe and an *s*, but placement isn't always that simple.

Let's examine how all three cases—nominative, objective and possessive—are used. It's a fast lesson!

NOMINATIVE CASE

When you think of the *nominative case,* think subjective. The subject of a verb, the complement of a linking verb (p. 17) or an appositive (related word, phrase or clause) are all in the nominative case.

<u>Meg</u> is an ambitious politician.
(subj.-noun)

<u>He</u> plunged into the icy waters of the reservoir.
(subj.-pron.)

It was <u>she</u> who signed the complaint.
(Complement of l.v.—pron. in nom. case)

<u>We</u> dreamers have to work, too.
(Pron. is appositive of subj. dreamers, stays in nom. case)

Obviously, the nominative case can be used more than once in a sentence: It can appear in every clause. Here is an example of a compound-complex sentence with pronouns serving as both a subject and a complement of a linking verb:

<u>We</u> printers must fight government repression at every turn; it is <u>we</u> who must oppose the Crown's cleverly disguised thievery.

As you recall from Chapter 2, there are nominative forms of personal pronouns and of one interrogative relative pronoun:

Personal Pronouns		**Interrogative Pronoun**
Singular	*Plural*	
I	we	who
you	you	
he/she/it	they	

USE OF NOMINATIVE WITH LINKING VERBS

Although use of personal pronouns in the nominative case should give you little trouble, you need to be aware that the nominative case is not always used in certain informal speech. The rule that a complement following a linking verb should be in the nominative case (for example, the grammatically correct "It is I") is not as entrenched as it might be. In fact, these sentences have been acceptable in colloquial speech for years:

It's me. That's him.

These sentences may sound better in the objective case simply because the pronoun complement of the subject is close to the verb. However, that does not ring true in all similar constructions. The sentence

It was <u>she</u> who broke the story.

might not sound right, but it is grammatically correct. The objective "feeling" of the pronoun that follows the linking verb *is* loses force because *she* is next to the subject of another clause—*who broke the story.* In this sentence, both good grammar and close sounding dictate that *she* stay in the nominative case. However, keep in mind that such a construction is not the paragon of clear, concise writing; it is more direct to say that

She broke the story.

or

Betty Ann Boeving, fresh out of journalism school, broke the story of the zoning scandal.

In any case, try to separate "rules" for informal, colloquial speech from those for formal, permanent writing. Although informal style is creeping into some writing, we suggest that you seek a ruling from your publication. We hope that the decision does not fall on the side of inflexible (and awkward) grammar.

SELECTING *WHO* IN COMPLEX CONSTRUCTIONS

Although there are similar pressures to make the *who/whom* choice more liberal, we believe that writers should be very careful in their selections. Most of us have little difficulty recognizing the correct use of *who* when it is the simple subject of a simple clause:

> The astronauts, <u>who</u> have been training for this mission for three years, were understandably disappointed about the mission's cancellation.

But when the true subject *who* is separated from its clause, there is a tendency to use the objective case incorrectly. Note this example:

> The adviser <u>who</u> (not whom) the president said had leaked the information was asked to resign.

Whom is not the object of *the president said.* The sentence can be analyzed this way:

> The adviser . . . was asked to resign
> (main clause)
>
> who . . . leaked the information
> (subordinate clause)
>
> the president said
> (parenthetical information)

As you recall from Chapters 3 and 4, you must match the number of the subject to the proper verb. It is also important to select the right case if your subject is a pronoun:

> <u>Who</u> did he say won the race?
> (*Who* won the race, he did say.)

WHO/WHOM IN PREPOSITIONAL PHRASES

A pronoun in a prepositional phrase normally is in the objective case because it is generally the object of a preposition, as in "for *whom* the bell tolls," or "to *whom* did you wish to speak?" (see p. 35). But that's not always true.

Sometimes a preposition acts as a linking device, much like a conjunction or a relative pronoun. Look to the clause that follows to determine whether the pronoun is acting as subject or object:

I want to meet with <u>whoever</u> charged this pizza delivery to my account.

Although the object of a preposition normally takes the objective case, the presence of an entire clause connected to the preposition changes all the rules. All clauses need a subject, either stated or implied. Hence, we use *whoever* in the preceding sentence. The nominative choice is clearer when the sentence is rewritten for analysis:

<u>Whoever</u> charged their pizza delivery to my account has to meet with me immediately.

Here's another example:

He discussed the end of the world with <u>whoever</u> would listen.

Note the two clauses:

<u>He</u> discussed/<u>whoever</u> would listen.
(subj.)   (subj.)

CASE IN *THAN* CLAUSES

Beware of comparative *than* clauses when selecting case.

He is smarter than <u>I</u>.

Than is frequently a conjunction. As you'll recall, conjunctions connect whole clauses and phrases. Because the second clause in a comparison is sometimes implied, you must mentally complete the thought to determine proper case:

He is smarter than <u>I</u> (am smart).

In this sentence, the nominative case *I* is required because that pronoun is the subject of the implied clause.

However, *than* can also be a preposition.

There is no better bungee-jumper than <u>her</u>.

You can see that *than* is not a conjunction here because in this sentence, the comparison ends with *her*. Tacking on "than she is a bungee-jumper" doesn't make sense because the writer is actually expressing a superlative, not a comparative.

OBJECTIVE CASE

Personal pronouns and the pronoun *who* also change form when used in the objective case:

Personal Pronouns		Interrogative Pronoun
Singular	*Plural*	
me	us	whom
you	you	
him/her/it	them	

THE PERSONAL PRONOUN IN THE OBJECTIVE CASE

You can use personal pronouns in the objective case in the following ways:

• As the direct or indirect object of a verb or verbal.

The warden led <u>him</u> to the execution site.
(dir. obj.)

The proud veteran showed <u>her</u> the <u>campaign medals</u>.
(indir. obj.) (dir. obj.)

Surprising Betty and <u>him</u> during the burglary
(obj. of ger.)
proved fatal to the Smiths.

"Surprising Betty and him" is a gerund phrase that acts as the complete subject of the sentence. However, "Betty and him" is the object of the gerund (receives the so-called action of the gerund), and therefore must be in the objective case.

• As the object of a preposition.

<u>Between</u> you and <u>me</u>, this play will close in a week.
(prep.)

- As the appositive of any word in the objective case.

   She gave the painting job to <u>us</u> boys.
   (appositive)

   Security guards dragged <u>us</u> reporters out of the convention hall.
   (appos.)

THE PROPER USE OF *WHOM*

The relative and interrogative pronoun *who* changes its form to *whom* in the objective case. The *who/whom* choice is one of the more confusing ones in grammar, but it is easier to make if you analyze the sentence properly. Let's look at these examples:

1. <u>Whom</u> did the <u>speaker</u> name to chair the committee?
   (dir. obj.)   (subj.)

   Keep in mind that a direct object need not follow the subject. It can appear before the subject, as in the preceding sentence. This grammatical rerouting should not be troublesome if you analyze the sentence more conventionally:

   <u>Speaker did name whom</u> to chair the committee.

2. She is the representative <u>whom</u> the speaker named to chair the committee.

   Identifying two subjects, two verbs, one complement and a direct object in this complex sentence helps you select *whom,* not *who.*

   <u>She</u>   <u>is</u>   the <u>representative</u>
   (subj.) (l.v.)   (complement)
   the <u>speaker</u> <u>named</u> <u>whom</u> to chair the committee
            (subj.) (verb)   (dir. obj.)

3. The caucus didn't know <u>whom</u> to appoint to the steering committee.

   In this case, it's simplest to read *whom to appoint* as the entire direct object of this sentence and *whom* as the simple object of *appoint.* It is also helpful to know that pronouns in an infinitive phrase almost never take the nominative case.

Are you going <u>to challenge him</u> in a runoff election?

A final example for this section:

Do you know <u>whom</u> to contact in the event of a grammatical crisis?

POSSESSIVE CASE

The *possessive* case is less troublesome than the nominative and objective. In this discussion, let's concentrate on three areas: the form and use of pronouns as possessives, nouns as possessives and the misuse of descriptive nouns as possessives.

FORM AND USE OF POSSESSIVE PRONOUNS

Personal pronouns have these possessive forms:

my, mine, our, ours, your, yours

his, her, hers, its, their, theirs

Note that an apostrophe is not needed with the possessive personal pronoun. However, some indefinite pronouns, such as *anyone, one, everyone, everybody, another* and *someone,* do require apostrophes in the possessive form.

Is this <u>my</u> book?
(modifies noun)

No, it is <u>mine.</u>
(represents noun)

Is this <u>your</u> book?
(modifies noun)

No, it is <u>yours.</u>
(represents noun)

Note also:

<u>One's</u> reach should exceed her grasp.

This is <u>everyone's</u> problem, believe me.

When a personal pronoun precedes a gerund in a sentence, the possessive case is needed because it shows possession or ownership by the gerund, which as you will recall always acts as a noun.

I don't understand <u>your</u> asking for an immediate transfer.

In this sentence, *your* modifies the gerund *asking.* Because a gerund is a noun, it is proper to use its pronoun in the possessive case. If you insert *request* in place of *asking,* you can more easily see its role as a noun in this sentence, as in

I don't understand <u>your request</u> for an immediate transfer.

The who-whose relationship

The relative pronoun *who* also has a possessive form: *whose.*

The Farm Security Administration tried in vain to relocate the farmer <u>whose</u> land had been ravaged by dust storms.

<u>Whose</u> car has enough gas to get to Milwaukee?

Note that the interrogative pronoun *who* also uses *whose* as its possessive form. *Who's* is a *contraction*—a compression of two words (*who is*). It is a subject and verb, not a possessive. Do not confuse *whose* and *who's.* If you can read *to whom* into a sentence with *whose* in it, your selection is probably correct.

<u>Whose</u> tofu is this?
(To whom does this tofu belong?)

<u>Who's</u> cooking the tofu tonight?
(Who is cooking . . . ?)

More about contractions

Contractions can also be troublesome with personal pronouns. Some of the most common errors involve misuse of *its/it's, your/you're* and *their/they're.*

The stock market soared to <u>its</u> highest point in history today.
(possessive)

The sportswriters think <u>it's</u> likely that Tech will win the championship.
(contraction of *it* and *is*)

<u>Your</u> ticket is at the box office.
(possessive)

<u>You're</u> going to love this new musical!
(contraction of *you* and *are*)

<u>Their</u> plans for the base camp did not consider
(possessive)
the possibility of avalanche.

<u>They're</u> getting ready to set up base camp.
(contraction of *they* and *are*)

You can add the expletive *there* to the *their/they're* confusion.

The junta announced <u>there</u> would be no elections until further notice.

<u>There's</u> a moon out tonight.

Or, to create a complete package:

<u>They're</u> convinced that <u>there</u> are no solutions to <u>their</u> problem.

Got it? We hope so!

NOUNS AS POSSESSIVES

When creating possessives for nouns, many writers get confused by the choice between an apostrophe and an apostrophe plus an additional *s*. They fear they don't know all the rules. True, there are a few rules, but they are not difficult. Here are eight simple ones, consistent with wire service style, for forming possessives of singular and plural nouns.

If a singular noun does not end in *s*, add *'s*.

the <u>accountant's</u> lack of humor

Joni <u>Mitchell's</u> lyrics

Old-line grammar books have ruled that nouns ending in *ce, x* or *z* (and carrying an *s* or *sh* sound) may carry an apostrophe at the end of the word without an *s*. However, many editors join us in asserting that most of these words can take an *'s*.

Hertz's management policies

science's need for research funding

the box's contents

Note, however, the exception in the following rule for those possessives that precede a word beginning with *s*.

If a singular common noun ends in *s*, add *'s* unless the next word begins with *s*. If the next word begins with *s*, add an apostrophe only. (This includes words with *s* and *sh* sounds.)

the boss's machine but the boss' stronghold

the witness's testimony but the witness' story

science's research priorities but for science' sake

If a singular proper noun ends in *s*, add an apostrophe only.

Yeats' poetry   Tom Robbins' novels   Paris' cuisine

If a noun is plural in form and ends in an *s*, add an apostrophe only, even if the intended meaning of the word (such as mathematics) is singular.

poems' meanings   witches' executions   measles' misery

mathematics' theorems   Marine Corps' spirit

If a plural noun does not end in *s*, add *'s*.

children's rights   oxen's yoke   media's transgressions

If there is joint possession of a noun, use the correct possessive form for the possessive closest to that noun.

Tracy and Hepburn's romance

her husband and <u>children's</u> future

Katherine and <u>Charles'</u> sailboat

If there is separate possession of the same noun, use the correct possessive form for each word.

<u>Morrison's</u> and <u>Robbins'</u> novels

<u>Tanzania's</u> and <u>Paraguay's</u> allies

In a compound construction, use the correct possessive form for the word closest to the noun. Avoid possessives with compound plurals.

Society of <u>Friends'</u> magazine

<u>father-in-law's</u> intransigence

Postal <u>Service's</u> rate hike

<u>attorney general's</u> opinion

DESCRIPTIVE NOUNS: NO POSSESSION NEEDED

Rather than using an adjective to modify a noun, writers often pair nouns as a descriptive tool. In these instances, the possessive form is not needed because the writer does not want to stress ownership.

Descriptive Nouns	Possessive Nouns
<u>government</u> policy	our <u>government's</u> priorities
<u>wine</u> cellar	a <u>wine's</u> bouquet
<u>citizens</u> band radio	<u>citizen's</u> arrest

It can be appropriate to join two nouns for the purposes of description, but it will not always work. Sometimes the attempt results in awkward phrasing as in:

a police report on race harassment.

Police, as a noun, works smoothly with the other noun, *report.* However, you can see the awkwardness with the noun *race* when an available adjective can work much better:

a police report on <u>racial</u> harassment

In that same vein, *Congress budget appropriations* doesn't flow in the way that the adjective *Congressional* would with the paired nouns.

Obviously, it is weak writing to link too many nouns together for descriptive purposes. Some writers may think that this creates tighter writing, but it's a false economy. Further, poorly glued constructions like "Bruin basketball team booster club" and "union-management negotiation procedure analysis" only serve to sabotage sentence clarity.

Although you may understand the rules of possession, you should be aware of a number of exceptions to these rules in the stylebooks of various publications and wire services. These guides are intended to create consistency of usage for their publications and services; in most cases, you will find them very helpful.

CHAPTER 6

Passive Voice

Passive: *unresponsive, dronish, bland, feeble.* Look up the word in your dictionary or thesaurus, and this is what you'll find. Are these the adjectives you'd like attached to your writing? *Parasitic, listless, unassertive, stagnant.* Read on. The list of synonyms continues: *sluggish, leaden, torpid, bovine.* Bovine? Imagine cowlike prose, spiritless, thick-witted, cud-chewing sentences standing around dull-eyed and cloddish. If you had the choice between writing direct, forthright, energetic prose or *bovine* prose, which would you choose?

Good. That settled, let's learn how to keep the cows in the barn where they belong.

> Awkwardness is caused when passive voice is used. Power is robbed from sentences, and stiltedness is caused. Strong verbs are weakened.

> When writers use passive voice, they create awkward prose and powerless, stilted sentences with weakened verbs.

Read the first example again. Do you hear the mooing and cud chewing? Does the language sound clumsy and unnatural? We think so. This is passive voice construction at work. Now read the second example, with the ideas rewritten in the active voice. If you can recognize the improvement—the leaner construction, the faster pace, the straightforward design, the strong, unencumbered verbs—then you know why active voice is almost always preferable.

WHAT IS PASSIVE VOICE?

Voice refers to the form of the verb. The subject acts when you use the *active voice* verb form. In *passive voice*, the person or thing performing the action becomes the object of the sentence. It does not act; it is acted on by the verb.

Volunteers from the neighborhood painted the house. (active)

The house was painted by volunteers from the neighborhood. (passive)

The house was painted. (passive)

In the first sentence, the actor (*volunteers*) is performing the action (*painted*) on the recipient (*house*). In the second sentence, the recipient (*house*) is having the action (*painted*) performed on it by the actor (*volunteers*). The second sentence is an awkward inversion of the first. Look at it this way:

Active Construction

who	did what	to whom
actor	performed action	on recipient
volunteers	painted	house

Passive Construction

who	had what done to it	by whom
recipient	acted on	by actor
house	was painted	by volunteers

The third sentence is also in the passive voice. Here the actor—*who* painted the house—is missing. The recipient (*house*) is being acted on (*painted*), but we do not know by whom.

Unless something else is wrong with a passive voice sentence, it is not technically a grammatical error. In fact, all three of the example sentences are grammatically correct. But whereas the first sentence is lean and straightforward, the second is clumsy and stilted. The third does not do the job we expect of a good sentence. It does not tell us all the information.

Some novice writers mistakenly think the presence of *is, was* or another form of the verb *to be* necessarily signals the passive voice. Although passive voice construction does use *to be* forms, not all *to be* forms are passive voice.

She was playing trombone in the band. (active)

Here the actor (*she*) performs the action (*was playing*). The order is straightforward: who did what to whom. The *was* does not signal passive voice. It is merely a helping or auxiliary verb. For this sentence to be in the passive voice, it would have to be constructed like this:

In the band, the trombone was played by her. (passive)

Note that *trombone*, the recipient of the action, is now the subject of the sentence. The actor, *she*, which was the subject of the first sentence, now appears as the object *her*. The order is inverted; the result is clumsiness.

In the following sentence, *was* does signal a passive voice construction:

He was mugged. (passive)

This sentence is passive because *he* is the recipient of the action, not the one performing the action. The actor, the person responsible for the mugging, is absent from the sentence.

He was mugged by an out-of-work novelist. (passive, actor supplied)

An out-of-work novelist mugged him. (active)

Don't try to identify passive voice by the tense of the verb or by the presence of auxiliary verbs. Instead, find the verb and ask: Who or what is performing this action? If the actor (the *who*) is missing, or if the actor is having the action performed on it rather than directly doing the action, then the sentence is passive.

Take another look at the first sentence of the two examples near the beginning of this chapter:

Awkwardness is caused when passive voice is used.
(*Who/what* causes awkwardness? *Who* uses passive voice?)

When writers use passive voice, they create awkward prose.
(Active voice; *who* does *what* to *whom*)

Now that you can identify passive voice, let's consider its major disadvantages.

DISADVANTAGES OF PASSIVE VOICE

1. Passive voice tends to sap the verb of its power. Partially, this is because of the presence of an auxiliary verb (a form of the verb *to be*) followed by a preposition (usually *by*). But it is also because the relationship between action and actor is indirect rather than straightforward.

    The speech was booed by angry workers. (passive)

    Angry workers booed the speech. (active)

    Passive voice can also bury the real verb of the sentence. Look at what happens to the strong, direct verb *accused* in the following sentences:

    The governor accused the press of sensationalism. (active)

    Accusations were made by the governor about sensationalism in the press. (passive)

    The passive voice sentence changes the verb *accused* to the noun *accusations*. The result is stilted construction and a flabby sentence.

2. Passive voice can make a sentence unnecessarily awkward by reversing the expected "who did what to whom" relationship. Subject-verb-object is almost always the clearest, smoothest construction. It is also the most succinct. Changing the order means adding unnecessary words.

    Hepatitis was contracted by dozens who ate at Bo's Big Burgers last month. (passive, awkward)

Dozens who ate at Bo's Big Burgers last month contracted hepatitis. (active)

3. Passive voice creates false formality. It can make a sentence sound impersonal, bureaucratic and overinflated.

It has been shown by numerous studies that tanning can prematurely age and damage your skin. (passive, unnecessarily formal)

Numerous studies show that tanning can prematurely age and damage your skin. (active)

Tanning can prematurely age and damage your skin, according to numerous studies. (active)

The tendency to use passive voice to create formality may come from term paper writing or textbook reading, where such overblown sentences often reside. As a favorite construction of politicians and scientists, passive voice is all around us. But as writers we must strive to communicate simply, directly and unpretentiously.

4. Passive voice may intentionally or accidentally obscure *who* or *what* is responsible for an action. It can hide the identity of the actor from your audience.

Mistakes were made.

Who made these mistakes? The passive voice construction masks the identity of the responsible entity. But *who* or *what* is responsible for an action might be the most vital information. How are we to understand the real meaning behind this sentence if the actor is obscured? Consider the vastly different implications of the following sentences:

"Mistakes were made," the president said at his morning press conference.

"I made mistakes," the president admitted at his morning press conference.

The inclusion of *who* makes a difference, doesn't it?

CORRECTING PASSIVE VOICE

Unless you have a specific reason to use passive voice (see p. 91), avoid it by constructing or rewriting sentences in the active voice. Remember, in the active voice, the actor performs the action. That doesn't mean that all sentences will be alike. You can vary sentences by placement of phrases and clauses, by length, by internal rhythm or by any number of other stylistic decisions.

Correcting passive voice is simple once you recognize the construction. Here's how:

1. Find the verb in the sentence.

2. Ask yourself *who* or *what* is performing the action of the verb. When you do this, you are identifying the actor in the sentence. Keep in mind that some passive voice sentences omit the real actor. You may not be able to find the person or thing responsible for the action in the sentence; you may have to add it.

3. Construct the sentence so that the real actor performs the action.

Now let's go through the three steps, beginning with the following passive voice sentence:

The movie rights to the book were sold for $4 million by a 22-year-old, first-time agent.

1. The verb is *were sold*.

2. *Who* performed the action? *Who* sold? *The agent.* He or she should be the subject of the sentence.

3. Constructing the sentence so that the actor performs the action, we get:

A 22-year-old, first-time agent sold the movie rights to the book for $4 million.

WHEN PASSIVE VOICE IS JUSTIFIED

Because passive voice construction reverses the order of a sentence from actor-verb-recipient to recipient-verb-actor, it is a useful and justifiable construction when (1) the recipient is more important than the actor or (2) the actor is unknown, irrelevant or impossible to identify.

1. In certain instances, the recipient of the action is more important (in journalism, more *newsworthy*) than the performer of the action.

   A priceless Picasso was stolen from the Metropolitan Museum of Art yesterday by three men posing as janitors.

   The verb is *stolen*. Who *stole*? The three men. But clearly what was stolen—the painting—takes precedence in the sentence. It is, at least until the men are identified or apprehended, the most newsworthy element in the sentence. Passive voice is justified in this instance.

   A trio of 10-year-old girls was arrested last night after a shoplifting spree that netted them more than $1,000 worth of soccer equipment and Barbie dolls.

   The verb is *arrested*. *Who* arrested? The sentence does not tell us. The person or persons performing the action in the sentence is missing. But because arrests are almost always made by law enforcement personnel, the actor is far less important than the recipient of the action—the girls who were arrested. Passive voice is allowable, even preferable, in this example as well.

2. Sometimes the *who* or *what* performing the action is unknown or is difficult to identify. When the doer cannot be identified, the writer has little choice but to construct a passive voice sentence. In this case, passive voice is appropriate.

   The cargo was damaged during the trans-Atlantic flight.

   The verb is *damaged*. *Who* or *what* damaged the cargo? Air turbulence? Temperature change? An escaped pet in the cargo hold? The doer of this action is unknown. The recipient of the action—what was damaged—assumes the prominent place in the sentence.

   Occasionally, an expert writer might use passive voice as a stylistic device to create a sense of detachment, a sense that no one is taking responsibility for certain actions, a feeling that actions are out of control or mysterious. Purposefully obscuring or taking away prominence from the doer might create suspense. Passive voice as a stylistic element, used conservatively and appropriately, might be useful in short stories, essays, an occasional magazine feature or even in advertising copy.

SHIFTING VOICES

Do not change voice from active to passive, or vice versa, within a sentence. This muddled construction shifts focus and confuses your audience. Active voice emphasizes the doer. Passive voice emphasizes the recipient.

> **Student protesters expressed concern over higher tuition costs, but the lack of affordable insurance was not mentioned at yesterday's rally.**

The focus of the first part of the sentence is *student protesters,* the doers or actors. The focus of the second part of the sentence is *affordable insurance* (the recipient of the action *was not mentioned*), resulting in a confusing and awkward shift. It adds unnecessary words and robs the second verb, *mentioned,* of its power. The sentence would be stronger and clearer if both parts were in the active voice.

> **Student protesters expressed concern over higher tuition costs but did not mention the lack of affordable insurance at yesterday's rally.**

Shifts to the passive are particularly common after an impersonal *one* or *you:*

> **If you study harder, grades can be improved.**

The first part of the sentence is in active voice. The second part shifts the emphasis from the actor (*you*) to the recipient (*grades*). Keep both sentence parts in active voice for clarity:

> **If you study harder, you can improve your grades.**

A FINAL WORD

Active voice creates sharp, clear, vigorous sentence construction. It is straightforward and powerful. Be active—and direct—unless you have a justifiable reason to use passive voice. Keep those cows in the barn.

CHAPTER 7

Punctuation

As dictionaries and stylebooks will tell you, *punctuation* is an important tool. Both hammer and file, it helps us build and shape. We also like to think of punctuation as one of the artist's brushes. Indeed, when you add a period or a comma to a sentence, you apply an artisan's finish to the work, clarifying meaning, emphasizing a point or regulating the flow of the thought.

Some editors, like the late, legendary Theodore Bernstein of the *New York Times*, likened punctuation marks to traffic signals: They say stop, pause, abruptly break for another thought, interpret this as a question.

It may also be helpful to think of punctuation marks in terms of the guidance they provide to sound or meter. For example, try reading this rambling construction aloud:

Why did you have to go after so many years together we've proved we can survive anything haven't we

The use of punctuation marks can vary in this construction; how you use them affects the meter (and the sound) of such arrangements:

Why did you have to go? After so many years together, we've proved we can survive anything. Haven't we?

Or try this version:

Why did you have to go after so many years together? We've proved we can survive anything, haven't we?

Or this:

Why did you have to go after so many years? Together, we've proved we can survive anything—haven't we?

The punctuation marks we choose will guide the flow and in some cases the intensity of our words. We can't write without them; we certainly would spoil our creative work if we used them incorrectly.

Let's examine a quick summary of our marks of punctuation:

- A *period* ends a sentence.

- A *comma,* however, creates only a pause.

- A *semicolon* slows the reader down; however, it isn't strong enough to stop anyone.

- A *colon* tells us the following: You're about to read a list, be introduced to a fragment or a sentence or be given a quotation to read.

- A *dash*—maligned by purists but used frequently in journalism—creates a more abrupt break than the comma.

- *Quotation marks* are "busy beavers." They are used to record speech faithfully, signify book titles and point attention to nicknames, among other things.

- A *hyphen* is well-used in our language. It creates economy by joining modifiers that belong together.

- *Ellipses* warn us . . . something is missing.

- *Parentheses* (they look like this) are used to add needed information without harming sentence rhythm.

- Do you really need an explanation of the *question mark?*

- Of course not! Ditto for the *exclamation mark!*

The apostrophe has been discussed in detail in Chapter 5, where possessives and contractions were reviewed.

Although there are styles and fads in punctuation, we writers must deal with logical, consistent rules. Clarity is at stake—we can leave creative punctuation to poets, who essayist Donald Hall says are "notoriously innovative." Writer Paul Robinson tells us that punctuation, like other areas of grammar, undergoes many changes:

> A single page of Thomas Carlyle, or any 19th-century writer, reminds us, for instance, that a comma between subject and verb—for me the most offensive of all punctuation errors—was once perfectly acceptable.

Media writers thrive on consistency. A set of well-defined rules gives that stability. Of course, these rules assume that you understand sentence construction. For a review, please consult Chapter 3.

PERIOD

As the most terminal of all punctuation marks, the period signals the end point of a statement. It makes us stop, not pause. Imagine how difficult it would be to read a sentence with internal periods:

> More than 400 searchers. threatened with a methane explosion. continued to search for survivors. of the mine cave-in.

That rhythm may be fine for a telegram (in fact, it was a feature of the Civil War-era newspaper headline), but readers won't hang on for long.

Lack of the period also harms meter, creating the dreaded run-on, which you can see is actually two sentences desperately in need of a period:

> Rescue officials could not determine whether anyone had been trapped in the cave-in searchers continued to work through the night under the threat of another methane explosion.

Because of the need for meter (flow and rhythm) and the need to stop readers before they move on to another thought, we use the period. The period actually has two main uses in writing.

Use a period to end a sentence that is neither interrogative (?) nor exclamatory (!).

> The coach asked the referee whether he'd like a loan to buy a Seeing Eye dog.

> Use a period to create certain abbreviations and to indicate decimals.

<u>Gov.</u> Richards has vetoed the $<u>17.5</u> million highway bill.

Abbreviations are space savers. Periods help signal these shortcuts. However, not all abbreviations require periods. *Acronyms* (abbreviations without punctuation, which are pronounceable words—for example, UNESCO), names of certain organizations and government agencies (NBC, UAW, FBI, CIA) and abbreviations of technical words (mph, rpm)—do not require periods. To learn which abbreviations use periods and which ones don't, consult your publication's stylebook or a dictionary.

COMMA

The comma's use to create a pause is mainly for clarity. Ironically, however, clarity suffers when confusion arises over the comma's placement. The comma can also be used to excess, prompting many editors to caution against overdependence.

Let's examine proper use of the comma and then look at some of its inappropriate uses.

> Use commas to separate items in a series.

Fire Marshal Tom Jefferson said the blaze could have been caused by defective wiring, a chemical reaction in a mixing tank or arson.

The forecast calls for light showers, some clearing and morning fog.

The rule that controls the so-called serial comma is this: When the last item in a series is connected by a coordinating conjunction (*and, or, but, nor, for, yet, so*), the comma can be omitted before that conjunction. This is especially true when the series is short or uncomplicated.

However, if the series is longer, the comma can be inserted before the conjunction to eliminate confusion:

Union officials this morning said they would bargain vigorously for the right to determine pension fund <u>investments, for</u> an expanded procedure of grievance <u>settlements, and for</u> binding arbitration of all contract matters not settled within 90 days of the start of negotiations.

We should note that the elimination of the serial comma is particularly favored in journalistic writing. It is used more frequently in formal composition, and it's not unusual to have use of the serial comma emphasized in the teaching of standard English.

Use a comma to separate two independent clauses connected by a coordinating conjunction, as long as the clauses don't contain much internal punctuation.

Seven men were arrested this morning at a methamphetamine "factory" on the east <u>side, and</u> three more were taken into custody six hours later.

Volcanic activity continues on the <u>mountain, but</u> U.S. Forest Service officials said they will continue to issue climbing permits on a limited basis.

Remember that an independent clause can stand alone as a complete sentence. A compound predicate (two or more verbs that serve the same subject) does not need a comma because it is part of the same clause.

The <u>judge</u> <u>fined</u> the men $250 and
   (subj.) (verb)
<u>ordered</u> them to perform 40 hours
(verb)
of community service.
(Read as *the judge fined and ordered*—there is only one clause in this sentence.)

Journalistic style favors dropping the comma if both independent clauses of the sentence are short and if the sentence does not lose its meter.

The Assembly approved the bill but the governor vetoed it.

When in doubt, however, leave the comma in.

⬛ Use commas to set off long introductory clauses and phrases and some shorter clauses and phrases that would be confusing without the comma.

After the fire alarm went off for the third time that night, the hotel clerk finally called the fire department.

Every day, television viewers are asked to make sense of an increasingly jaded and complicated nation.

To Meryl Streep, Oscar is a familiar name.

You can omit the comma for some short clauses and phrases if no run-on occurs in the sentence—that is, if the meaning of the introductory segment remains distinct from the rest of the sentence. A comma is not necessary here:

For six nights floodwaters threatened the safety of Des Moines.

⬛ Use commas to set off nonrestrictive (nonessential) clauses, phrases and modifiers from the rest of the sentence.

Restrictive (essential)

Let's look first at what is essential to the meaning of a sentence. *Essential* clauses, phrases or words do not need to be set off from the rest of the sentence. They are *restrictive*.

Three men who tried to commandeer a city bus died when they attempted to flee from the hijacking.

The subordinate clause *who tried to commandeer . . .* limits the meaning of the sentence. One test to determine restrictive meaning is to read the sentence without the clause in question. If you find yourself trying to "fill in" the meaning of the sentence, that clause is essential. For example, in the preceding example:

Three men died when they attempted to flee from the hijacking.

clearly needs its accompanying clause to make the sentence more complete, more understandable. For this reason, that clause does not need to be set off by commas.

Another example:

> Soybean futures <u>that were sold in the last two weeks</u> have been voided by the Chicago Board of Trade.

Not all soybean futures have been voided, only a specific group of sales. Because the clause is essential to the meaning of the sentence, no comma is needed. Note that in a restrictive clause the pronoun *that* is used instead of *which.* If the clause is not essential to the meaning of the sentence and just provides added detail, use *which* and set off the clause with commas. See also the entry in Part Two for *that/which/who.*

> Groucho Marx's <u>brother Chico</u> was an orchestra leader later in his career.

Groucho had several other brothers—remember Harpo, Zeppo and Gummo? Using commas in the example to separate the subject brother from its appositive *Chico* would mean that he had only one brother. The absence of commas here reveals the necessity of the name *Chico* to the meaning of the sentence.

Nonrestrictive (nonessential)

Nonrestrictive clauses, phrases and words do need commas because they are *nonessential,* or incidental, to the sentence. Look at these examples and see how they differ from the restrictive constructions.

> Edwards, <u>who will turn 75 tomorrow,</u> will appear before the parole board to argue that 15 years of a 25-year sentence is sufficient punishment for his robbery conviction.

This sentence does not depend on the underlined subordinate clause to complete its meaning. Other nonessential, amplifying pieces of information could have been added, such as *who has consistently maintained his innocence.*

> Potato Cellar Vineyards, <u>which is one of Idaho's oldest wineries,</u> won a gold medal for this year's bottling of Pinot Gris.

The subordinate clause about the age of the winery does not have a necessary connection to news of the award. It is not essential.

> Sam Bradley, <u>the Sioux City spitballer of Boston Braves fame,</u> died last night at 78.

The underlined phrase is called an *appositive,* a word or phrase that further defines the word that precedes it. It is not essential to the sentence but adds greater information and context.

◥ **Use commas to separate descriptive modifiers of equal rank.**

When a noun is preceded by a string of adjectives, apply this two-part test to determine whether those adjectives need to be separated by commas: Can you use these adjectives interchangeably? Can you successfully insert the conjunction *and* between these adjectives and have the sentence make sense? If so, these adjectives (modifiers) are coordinate and require a comma.

Given that test, the modifiers in the following sentence would not need a comma:

Meteorologists forecast another <u>cold Midwestern</u> night.
(The noun *night* has two modifiers—*cold* and *Midwestern.* You can't read *cold and Midwestern night* into it, so the adjectives must be separated by a comma.)

When you add a coordinate modifier, the sentence changes:

Meteorologists forecast another <u>cold, dreary</u> Midwestern night.
(You can read *cold and dreary* into this sentence. They modify *Midwestern night* equally, so they are considered coordinate.)

These sentences show the proper use of commas:

Scientists cannot predict the next eruption of the <u>fickle, explosive</u> volcano.

The <u>vacant, cold</u> eyes of the rescue team revealed the depth of the Colombian earthquake.

◥ **Use commas to set off parenthetical expressions.**

A *parenthetical expression* is similar to a "theatrical aside." It is not part of the main (onstage) conversation but is intended to give extra information in a quieter tone. These statements could be put in parentheses, but that might be too formal and stilted. Use commas to create shorter pauses without disrupting the flow of the sentence.

These same council members, <u>you may recall,</u> voted themselves a 35-percent pay increase last year.

🔖 Use commas when the absence of a pause can cause confusion.

For the <u>senator, going fishing</u> is vacation enough.

Circling the <u>brewery, workers</u> kept a silent vigil to protest unsafe working conditions.

Although it is important not to overuse the comma, it would be a false economy to waive its use in the preceding two examples. The pause is necessary for clarity of the sentences.

🔖 Use commas to set off participial phrases that modify some part of the independent clause.

The Senate adjourned today, <u>having successfully defeated an attempt to call witnesses in the bark beetle scandal</u>.
(phrase modifies Senate)

Various stylebooks list many other examples of comma use. Some may be obvious to you.

1,250 votes—but 999 votes and 2450 Heavenly Drive

He lives in Wapakoneta, Ohio.

Ozzie, will you answer the door?

COMMA MISUSE

The comma can be as tempting as a bulging bag of crisp, salty potato chips: It's hard to stop at just one.

We know that the comma is meant to improve flow, not to obstruct it. However, poor construction and comma overuse often combine to create a form of literary stammering. Writers and editors must be careful to avoid excessive use of the comma. Here are some helpful rules to help you avoid comma overuse:

🔖 Do not use a comma to separate two independent clauses that are not joined by a coordinating conjunction.

Violating this rule produces the *comma splice,* one of the most common errors in punctuation. It looks like this:

The unemployment rate continues to <u>drop, the</u> rate of inflation is staying constant.

Using a comma to link two independent clauses (which could stand alone as two sentences) does not help sentence flow and clarity. We recommend that you break the sentence in two, or you can do two other things:

- Use a semicolon to link the clauses.

  The unemployment rate continues to <u>drop; the</u> rate of inflation is staying constant.

- Use a coordinating conjunction with a comma.

  The unemployment rate continues to <u>drop, but</u> the rate of inflation is staying constant.

> Do not use a comma to introduce a subordinate clause.

The use of a comma before the conjunction *because* is one of the biggest offenders. *Because* introduces a dependent clause. It is not a coordinating conjunction; it does not join two clauses of equal rank. *Because* helps explain a statement in the main clause.

The mayor inspected the crash site <u>because she</u> needed a first-hand report.

No comma is needed here because the conjunction does not coordinate equal clauses. (Did you notice the lack of a comma in the previous sentence as well?) That is why *and, but* and *or* often require commas; they are called *coordinating conjunctions* because they link clauses of equal weight. (See Chapter 2 under "Conjunctions" for a listing of conjunctions that do not coordinate.)

Note that if the subordinate clause is being used to introduce the sentence, a comma is required:

Because she needed a firsthand <u>report, the</u> mayor inspected the crash site.

◣ Do not use a comma to separate a noun or pronoun from its reflexive.

A *reflexive* is any of the "self" pronouns (*myself, himself*) used to intensify or accent the noun or pronoun preceding it. A comma is not needed to set off the reflexive:

Meriwether himself will lead the next phase of the expedition.

◣ Do not use a comma between a word and a phrase that amplifies it if it will create a "false series."

This sentence, as punctuated, is bound to cause confusion:

Rescuers discovered seven bodies, six transients and one firefighter.

Unless the writer meant to say that 14 people were discovered and that seven of them were dead, the comma after *bodies* is wrong. A colon or dash would be more effective in separating the two ideas:

Rescuers discovered seven bodies—those of six transients and one firefighter.

◣ Do not use a comma to precede a partial quotation.

The mayor charged that his election opponent is "a charlatan of the lowest order."

No comma is needed because the quoted material is the predicate nominative of the verb *is*. Because the quoted material is dependent on the rest of the sentence for its context, that material need not be set off by a comma.

If the quotation is a full sentence, however, it should be preceded by a comma:

The public defender asked, "How would you like to be sent to prison for a crime you didn't commit?"

A good writer uses the comma for clarity and meter. If your sentences contain traffic jams of commas, review them. Perhaps they are too long and too busy. Be brief, be crisp; be sparing in your use of the comma.

SEMICOLON

The semicolon is a curious but effective mark of punctuation. It is half comma, half period. It indicates more than a pause; it is a break but not a stop. It is more inflexible than the comma or period; it carries a grammatical formality that some writers would just as soon avoid in their work. For this reason, perhaps, the semicolon is used infrequently in newswriting.

Writers sometimes opt for two separate and shorter sentences rather than joining two independent clauses with a semicolon. They may choose to break up a series of thoughts normally punctuated by semicolons to avoid long clauses and phrases.

Their hesitance to use the semicolon shows their dependence on the period. They equate the "full stop" with simplicity and clarity. The semicolon apparently doesn't project that image.

Used properly, the semicolon has three important assignments.

Use a semicolon to join independent clauses not connected by a coordinating conjunction.

The fire roared through the abandoned <u>warehouse; its</u> rapid progress was aided by several piles of gasoline-soaked rags.

If those two clauses had been connected with the coordinating conjunction *and*, a comma would have sufficed:

. . . warehouse, and its rapid . . .

Some writers prefer the use of the coordinating conjunction because it gives more specific direction to the reader. Others would look at these two long clauses and break them into two sentences.

It's important to note that words like *however, moreover, nevertheless* and *therefore* are not coordinating conjunctions. They are *conjunctive adverbs*. They do not coordinate clauses of equal rank. When one of them separates two independent clauses, a semicolon is required.

"This budget is <u>tentative; however,</u> I would be less than honest if I didn't reveal that we have enough votes to adopt it," Baker told the board.

As we mentioned earlier in the "Comma Misuse" section, using a comma here to separate the two clauses would create a comma splice. Semicolons also are needed when more than two independent clauses are linked in a series—even when the last part of the series is connected by a coordinating conjunction.

We must provide adequate funding for our <u>schools; we</u> cannot abandon our commitment to greater access to higher <u>education; and</u> we will press forward on our new income tax measure to fully fund our programs.

Use a semicolon to separate internally punctuated independent clauses joined by a coordinating conjunction.

When you punctuate a clause internally with commas, you can't use a comma to separate that clause from another. A semicolon is needed to create a more abrupt stop:

The Klansmen, who have promised that more than 50,000 members would join the march, threatened today to parade through the predominantly African-American area of Columbus; shortly after that announcement, city officials withdrew the group's assembly permit.

Now that's a lengthy (but not incomprehensible) sentence. Crisp, focused news style often compels you to break this construction into several sentences.

Use a semicolon to set off parts of a series that also contain commas.

Killed in the early morning collision were Aaron Jepsen, 37, of Brookings; his wife, Rhona, 32; their children, Tom, 12; Betty, 9; and Richard, 4.

The main function of the semicolon here is organization. It tidies up elements of a series so that they remain distinct.

We believe the semicolon is helpful when it clarifies boundaries in a series containing commas. But we urge you to avoid using the semicolon to connect two independent clauses. If you must use it, be sure that the two clauses actually need some connection and that they wouldn't be better off as separate sentences. Don't write

> The car slid off the roadway into the muddy embankment; the police arrived hours later to find that no one had survived

when you could write

> The car slid off the roadway into the muddy embankment. When police arrived hours later, they found three bodies crushed by the overturned vehicle.

As you can see, merging two strong thoughts into one construction can be economical, but it may not give you the completeness and creativity that two sentences can. Think of the semicolon as a clarifier, not an economizer.

COLON

The colon presents ideas with a flourish: It announces. It announces complete sentences, lists, quotations or dialogue.

PROPER USE OF THE COLON

When the colon is used to introduce a complete sentence, the first word of that sentence should be capitalized.

> Rock star Dewdrop Boysenberry has a bold idea: He will challenge wrestler Hulk Hogan for a congressional seat.

When a colon is used to introduce a word, phrase or clause that is not a complete sentence, the first word following the colon should not be capitalized.

> In the movie classic "The Graduate," Dustin Hoffman learned the one word that would guarantee his successful future: plastics.

Here are some other uses of the colon:

Use colons to introduce quotations that are longer than one sentence and to end paragraphs that introduce quotations in the next paragraph.

The judge eyed the defendant and told him in words dripping with disdain: "Your disgusting conduct in my courtroom has mocked everything that is justice. Please accept our jail hospitality for the next 45 days."

Here is the text of the president's speech:

"Good evening, my fellow Americans . . . ."

Use colons to show the text of questions and answers.

This can take two forms:

Q: And then what happened?

A: She put the meat cleaver down and called the cops.

Sneed: Senator, I have done my best to contribute to this discussion.

Ervin: Somebody told me once when I was representing a case; he said, "You put up the best possible case for a guilty client!"

As you can see, use of the colon eliminates the need to use quotation marks unless the dialogue itself quotes other material.

Use colons to show times and citations.

She ran the 5,000 meters in 15:02.

Psalm 101:5 tells us of the danger of slander.

WHEN NOT TO USE THE COLON

You do not need the colon if you are introducing a short list without the words *the following.*

The senate committee decided to interview Larry, Curly and Moe.

You do not need a colon when introducing a direct quotation of one sentence or less. A comma is sufficient.

What do you think of the slogan, "Just Do It"?
(Note the placement of the question mark outside the quotation marks. See p. 114.)

DASH

Some cynics contend that journalists invented the dash—that item of punctuation longer than a hyphen, less formal than a colon and more direct than parentheses—to impress readers with information that needed to be abruptly introduced. Actually, the dash has been with us for a long time. In formal grammar its primary uses are to change direction and to create emphasis.

However, journalists can be rightfully accused of using the dash to excess or of using it when a comma, a colon or parentheses might be more skillfully employed. We believe the dash should be used sparingly because it is a startling mark of punctuation. If it is used too often, it loses its impact. Let's look at the two main uses of the dash in all writing.

Use the dash to end a sentence with a surprising or ironic element.

The tall, distinguished-looking man entered the country with a valid passport, two pieces of leather luggage, an expensive camera around his neck—and 16 ounces of uncut heroin in the heels of his alligator shoes.

You can see that a comma here would not be as effective in changing meter and warning the reader of a break in thought. Using this reasoning, you would not want a dash in this "less surprising" sentence:

Montana voters today approved a referendum to increase spending limits for welfare payments, health insurance and low-income housing subsidies.

That series is similar in theme. Adding a dash gives the sentence false drama.

Use a dash to set off a long clause or phrase that is in apposition to the main clause when it makes the information clearer and more distinctive.

The closing ceremonies of the Olympics—a dazzling spectacle of America through neon-colored sunglasses—started a marathon of self-congratulations at CNN.

A comma usually suffices in a shorter appositive that does not require an abrupt break.

Baker, the Mudhens' far-ranging outfielder, proved his mettle again today with a rifle throw that eliminated a scoring threat at the plate.

The dash could also be used to set off both parenthetical expressions and a series of items in the middle of a sentence. However, we recommend you make these uses rare and concentrate on the two main uses of the dash. The dash is supposed to be an infrequently used piece of punctuation. Make your reader take notice of it.

QUOTATION MARKS

Quotation marks have several identities. They can be a tool of truthfulness when they give a faithful reproduction of what was said. They can also be a weapon that belittles what was said. What impressions do quotation marks create in these sentences?

"I believe we can correct this situation," the bank manager said.
(This seems to be a straightforward reproduction of what was said.)

The bank manager said her office could correct the "situation."
(Placement of quotation marks around *situation* makes us suspicious. What is so strange about this so-called situation? If it is something different from a situation, why put it in quotation marks? Why not call it something else?)

You can change the flow and character of a sentence by the way you use quotation marks. Let's look at the appropriate use of this punctuation mark in writing and then see how other marks of punctuation are used with quotations.

PROPER USE OF QUOTATION MARKS

Use quotation marks to enclose direct quotations and dialogue.

"You must remove this blasphemous trash from your library shelves," the irate citizen told the board.

"Will you be there tomorrow?" he asked.

"I'll try," she said curtly.

"I need to see you."

"I'll try."

Avoid the unnecessary use of partial quotations. Sometimes a paraphrase will do. So, instead of:

Board President Ann Armes said completion of a third nuclear plant is necessary if "we are to maintain our high bond rating."

you might write:

Completion of a third nuclear plant is necessary to preserve the board's high bond rating, according to President Ann Armes.

The partial quotation works best if the language or style of what is quoted is distinctive or colorful. For example, it would be difficult to paraphrase this effectively:

Sen. Tony Meeker, R-Amity, compared the higher education system to a dinosaur that's "going to fall in the tarpits and become a fossil."

Avoid wrapping quotation marks around single words if their use results in an inaccurate representation. We generally put these marks around unfamiliar terms on first reference, around slang words and around words used sarcastically or ironically. But don't overdo it.

A wage freeze is in effect.

His luck ran into a "freeze" at the track.

Sara Baker's dreams are a $3 million business.

Tom Anderson's "dreams" have ruined those of elderly investors who spent their life savings on his worthless pyramid scheme.

Use quotation marks for titles of books, lectures, movies, operas, plays, poems, songs, speeches, television shows and works of art. Do not use these marks for names of magazines, newspapers, reference books or the Bible.

"The Powers That Be"

"Madame Butterfly"

"NYPD Blue"

But note:

The Akron Beacon-Journal

Vanity Fair

Oxford English Dictionary

Use quotation marks for nicknames.

John "The Duke" Wayne

"Stormin' Norman" Schwarzkopf

USE OF OTHER PUNCTUATION WITH QUOTATION MARKS

"Does the question mark go inside or outside?" One of the most frequent questions about quotation marks involves the placement of other punctuation marks with them. Like so many aspects of our grammar, that depends. (Remember, coping with uncertainty makes you stronger!)

Punctuation that goes inside quotation marks

A bit of dogma first:

The period and comma always go inside quotation marks.

Thomas said, "The workers are looking to us for a peaceful solution."

"I had to borrow bus money to get here," the unemployed steel-worker told the commissioners.

Question marks and exclamation marks go inside quotation marks if they are part of the quoted material.

The governor asked, "Do you believe that your quality of life has improved during my administration?"

"Give me my dignity!" the prisoner pleaded.

Punctuation that goes outside quotation marks

Question marks and exclamation marks go outside if they are not part of the quoted material.

Have you seen "I Saw What You Did Last Summer Part Twenty"?

No, I haven't read "The Tofu Diet Book"!

HYPHEN

Whereas the dash sets words apart, the hyphen brings them together. It is a tiny bridge that links words for compound constructions and modifiers. Unfortunately, the hyphen can be as frustrating as it is useful. If you use it to join words that need to work as a unit, and if you use it to avoid confusion, the hyphen will serve you well.

Use the hyphen to join compound modifiers that precede a noun unless that modifier is preceded by *very* or an *-ly* adverb.

Compound modifiers belong together. They are not part of a series of adjectives and adverbs that can separately describe the word they are modifying. The components of a compound modifier actually modify themselves as they describe the noun.

a good-natured person
(This is a compound modifier. *Good* doesn't modify *person*. It modifies the other modifier, *natured*. Together they modify *person*. The person is good-natured, not good and natured. Hence, we employ the hyphen.)

a <u>sluggish, unresponsive</u> economy

(This is not a compound modifier. The economy is both sluggish and unresponsive. *Sluggish* doesn't modify *unresponsive*. No hyphen is needed.)

If you can insert the conjunction *and* between the modifiers and make sense of the new construction, then you do not have a compound modifier. A *sluggish and unresponsive* economy sounds right, but a *good and natured* person does not. That should be your signal for a hyphen under this rule, unless the beginning of the compound modifier is *very* or an *-ly* adverb. These words are a clear signal to the reader that a compound modifier is coming. No hyphen is needed in these cases. But note:

very refined person
(remember rule about *very*)

heavily spiced recipe
(remember rule about *-ly* adverbs)

Most compound modifiers are also hyphenated when they follow a form of the linking verb *be*. In that sense, they continue to modify the subject. So, while it is proper to write

She is a well-read student.

this punctuation is also correct:

The student was well-read.

Be sure to make a distinction between a compound modifier and the same set of words that really doesn't modify anything. It will prevent the improper use of the hyphen.

Last-minute election returns put him over the top.

Last-minute modifies *election returns*. Note, however:

He filed for election in the last minute of registration.

Last minute is the object of the preposition *in*. *Last* only modifies *minute*.

Be sure to identify all parts of a compound modifier. For example, it's not a 30 *mile-per-hour* speed limit. It's a *30-mile-per-hour* speed limit.

Use the hyphen for certain prefixes and suffixes.

You'll need to consult a dictionary or stylebook in some cases. There are so many exceptions that you will never guess right all the time! For example, the Associated Press stresses this rule:

> Hyphenate between the prefix and the following word if the prefix ends in a vowel and the next word begins with the same vowel. (For example, *extra-attentive;* exceptions are *cooperate* and *coordinate*.) Also hyphenate between the prefix and the following word if that word is capitalized (such as *super-Republican*).

Prefixes that generally take a hyphen include *all-, anti-, ex-, non-* and *pro-*. If you check a dictionary or stylebook, however, you will find plenty of exceptions.

Use the hyphen for combinations when the preposition is omitted.

Elko-Pocatello train

a 149-22 rout

inflation-recession cycle

ELLIPSES

We use the ellipsis mark (. . .) to alert the reader that something original has been removed from quoted material, that the speaker has hesitated or faltered or that there is more material than is actually cited or used.

"We must fight this closure . . . we must save this factory."
(The original statement was, "We must fight this closure by a management that is bent on saving money with no regard for this town; we must save this factory." In the interest of economy and impact, the writer condensed this statement but preserved its accuracy.)

Facing the hostile audience, Baker tried to frame his thoughts. "Under these circumstances," he said, "I feel I can no longer serve this community as superintendent. I have tried my best . . . I have always wanted. . . ." Unable to continue, he left the crowded meeting.

Remember these rules about punctuation with the ellipsis:

Another period is needed with the ellipsis if it ends the statement.

"This is a sorrowful time for all of us. . . ."

Other punctuation marks, if needed, come after the quoted material but before the ellipsis.

"How would you feel? . . ."

"We can't stand for this! . . ."

PARENTHESES

The characteristics of journalistic writing—brevity, crispness and clarity—imply that parentheses are not welcome. However, there are times when parentheses can be used effectively. Two of the most common are to signify the addition of needed information and to mark an aside, or something incidental, to the main thought.

Caveat emptor ("let the buyer beware") is a war cry for consumer activists.

He arrived at the bank, only to find it was closed. (It closed every day at noon.)

If you find that parenthetical material is getting too long or too complicated, perhaps a rewrite is in order.

If the material inside the parentheses is not a complete sentence, put the period outside the parentheses.

She likes decaffeinated coffee (the cold-water extract type).

If the parenthetical material is a complete sentence, but it depends on the sentence around it for context, put the period outside the parentheses.

He whispered, "carpe diem" ("seize the day").

If the parenthetical material is a complete sentence and can stand alone, put the period inside the parentheses.

Roads were clear this morning despite last night's heavy snowfall. (Reports coming in to the paper said that the Department of Transportation had authorized overtime for three full crews.)

QUESTION MARK AND EXCLAMATION MARK

If you are asking a *direct question,* you must use the question mark.

What's next for Microsoft?

If your question is *indirect,* no question mark is needed.

The world wants to know what is happening in Iraq.

The exclamation mark should be used only to express a strong emotion or surprise. In most writing you probably will employ it only in direct quotation because of the exclamation's sensational nature.

For example, you should not punctuate a sentence like this:

Montana's population increased 1 percent this year!

Both the exclamation mark and the question mark should be included inside quotation marks if the exclamation or question is part of the quoted material.

In direct quotations, remember that the comma is not necessary if the exclamation mark or the question mark is part of the quoted material that precedes attribution.

"You can't make me testify!" the angry defendant screamed.

"Is this really the kind of government we want?" the senator asked.

Remember: Punctuation gives order and direction to your writing. It provides clarity, flow, emphasis—even drama. Use punctuation marks wisely and naturally to put finishing touches on your writing.

CHAPTER 8

Spelling

"English spelling contains thousands of excuses for rebuking children, for beating them, for imprisoning them after school hours, for breaking their spirits with impossible tasks."

—From a letter to *The Times of London* in 1906, written by dramatist George Bernard Shaw

Ah, the scourge and challenge of spelling. Thank goodness for computer spell-checking, right? Well, what do you think some nifty software would do with this poem?

Now spelling does knot phase me
It does knot bring a tier.
My pay purrs awl due glad den
With wrapped words fare as hear . . .

This is no 14th-century work. It's a contemporary effort, penned by an anonymous cynic who was distressed with computer spell-check programs. It also proves that these programs can't detect spelling errors when a correctly spelled word is improperly used. Read the first two lines again, now with correct spelling for the intended words:

Now spelling does not faze me
It does not bring a tear.

Although this bit of poetry (doggerel?) may seem whimsical, one of our colleagues recently complained that his computer spell-checker urged him to change the spelling of *Geronimo* to *Geranium*. So it goes in this world of seemingly autocratic software.

To give critics of English spelling their due, our language can be frustrating, indeed, especially with its many *homonyms* (differently spelled words that sound alike, such as *see/sea, meet/meat/mete* and *patients/patience*) and what appear to be just as many exceptions as rules. A number of famous people have complained about the unfairness of our spellings. Count among them our 26th president Teddy Roosevelt and Andrew Carnegie, the Scottish-born steel baron known for his generous endowment of many U.S. libraries. Col. Robert McCormick, publisher of the Chicago Tribune in the early 20th century, actually imposed spelling changes into the style guide of his newspaper. So, for a brief period that nonetheless distressed teachers across the land, *phantom* became *fantom* and *although* was transformed into *altho*.

But the true thorn in the side of orthographers was the dramatist Shaw, who in 1950 put his money where his mouth was and left most of his estate to a project known as the Simplified Spelling program, which ironically required a 42-letter alphabet.

With this bit of background, we hope you will understand that although our language is indeed dynamic, rules are also important. Of course, some change in spelling is inevitable; the English spelling of *colour* became, after our Revolutionary War, *color;* indeed, the creation of Webster's American Dictionary was itself a revolutionary act.

In our view, spelling problems are somewhat linked to comprehension and word-recognition difficulties. These problems also involve structural issues, some of which have to do with meaning and some of which are tied to the "look" of a word. With the popular success of linguist Steven Pinker's "The Language Instinct," we suppose there may be even more clamor for suggesting that spelling deficiencies are tied to genetics. We'll pass on that debate and offer instead an analysis of how spelling problems are created and then discuss how to improve spelling skills.

RECOGNIZING PROPER SPELLING
SEEING/IMPRINTING

It doesn't necessarily follow that serious readers are good spellers—but a steady diet of the printed word can't hurt. In an electronic age in which we hear far more words than we see, we have fewer opportunities to visualize words and to understand their meaning. When we don't "see" these words, our retention of them and their context suffers. For example, it helps to see the word *environment* because the *n* in *environ* (its root) is often not properly pronounced. Seeing the sentence

Our <u>environment</u> is in danger

helps us understand and see the construction of this subject. The same is true for two similar-sounding adjectives: *discreet* (meaning modest or prudent) and *discrete* (meaning distinct or separate). Seeing these words in the context of their use greatly helps the imprinting process:

Theirs was a <u>discreet</u> liaison.

This issue has three <u>discrete</u> parts.

Hearing these words as well can give us some context for their use, but visualization is key to completing our understanding and future proper use.

Making the correct choice between *stationary* (not moving) and *stationery* (writing material) may not seem difficult, as the two words are quite different in meaning. Yet, how often are they confused and therefore misspelled? Then there's the matter of *sweet* versus *suite*; as you can tell, this could become a very long list! Our advice: See the word. Note the organization of its letters. Link that to its meaning and use. When you do that, you won't get confused over the spelling and word use in this sentence:

The $40-a-day <u>suite</u> was a <u>sweet</u> deal.

PRONUNCIATION

Now listen to the difference in these sounds:

Pro-nouns' (pronounce) and *Pro-nun-see-á-shun* (pronunciation).

Hearing the proper pronunciation of these two words can actually help us "see" the difference in their spellings. Note the "ow" in *pronounce* and the "un" in *pronunciation* and it's likely that you won't mistakenly spell out *pronounciation*. Again, seeing these words helps our imprinting.

Consider these two words as well: *wreck* (pronounced *rek* with a soft *e*, meaning to destroy accidentally) and *wreak* (pronounced *reek* and meaning to inflict punishment or damage). Not understanding the proper pronunciation of a word and its meaning led to this erroneous headline:

Storm <u>wrecks</u> havoc on fishing village

Fortunately, the study of *phonics* (teaching reading and spelling with the sounds of speech) is returning to our elementary schools. There is even a best-selling computer program available for children, widely advertised on television. This should reinforce the contention that although some language can be acquired by intuition and by guesswork, serious understandings of what words mean, how they are used, how they are arranged in sentences and exactly how they are spelled are all directly related to in-depth instruction in phonics, reading and meaning.

PROOFREADING

In our experience, many weak spellers are not careful readers. They may be "skimmers." Therefore, they won't be alert to checking words that appear suspicious. They may not assume that a certain percentage of words that they use may be spelled incorrectly. And, worst of all, they don't (or won't) look up the word to check meaning and spelling.

Proofreading is a natural part of any editing process. This process requires close attention to one's writing—its content, meaning, structure and spelling. Our advice is not to count on spell-checkers or on another editor to detect spelling errors. We say: Live with your dictionary. Inhale it. Understand the look, meaning and sound of words.

IMPROVING SPELLING

We suggest that you focus your efforts at spelling improvement on these areas: sound, sense and structure. It's a nonthreatening approach, and it brings you closer to your language as well.

SOUND

"Sounding out" a word by breaking it into phonetic patterns and into its syllables can improve your sense of how the letters are organized into words. It's amazing how many words you can "sound out" without the aid of a dictionary—and still come up with the right spelling. However, using the pronunciation guides in a dictionary yields valuable lessons. For example, look at the following words, which all have the same -*ough* endings:

through   **cough**   **bough**
(throo)   (kôf)   (bow [sounding like *ow*])

One spelling, several sounds—it's another one of the "charms" of English spelling!

Looking up words also reveals how many syllables a word has and which syllable is accented. This provides a "fine tuning" of the word. Consider these two nouns:

desert (déz-urt)—barren wilderness

dessert (di-zúrt)—something sweet after a meal

Their differing pronunciations should help distinguish their difference in spellings. Naturally, exceptions always spoil the example, so in the interest of full disclosure, we admit that the verb *desert* (to abandon) is pronounced like the noun *dessert*. (Nothing's perfect, right?)

Examining syllables will also give you a keener ear for pronunciation. Here are two often-misspelled words, broken into their syllables:

di-lem-ma
(not two *l*s and one *m*)

sep-a-rate
(*sep* and *rate* are not separated by an *e*! Further, the *a* is sounded as an *ah*, not *urh*, which would indicate an *e*.)

Checking pronunciation also makes you aware of silent (but not invisible) letters that can foil your spelling. For example, the musical *chord* has a silent *h*, which makes it sound exactly like the material *cord*. The normal pronunciation of *government* does not reveal the hidden *n*; yet, in this case *govern* is an obvious root. The same goes for a hidden *r* in *surprise*, although there is no sensible root here that will assist you.

Sound may be a great help in unraveling and then putting together difficult words, but making sense of meaning also plays a key role.

SENSE

What does this word mean?

What is its proper use in a sentence?

Answering these questions often requires the use of a dictionary, or at least a closer examination of the word. A special dividend of such a search is that you will see the correct spelling of the word. When you see certain word pairs together, perhaps you immediately understand the differences in their meanings—and spellings. But you would rarely see them together; so it helps to set up pairs (even trios) and study them with an eye toward their spelling differences.

Look at the following combinations. They are all homonyms (words that sound alike but that have different spellings.) You probably can define the differences between many of them, but how quickly can you adjust to their different spellings? That part of seeing—and understanding—a word, especially in the context of a sentence, is critical to the proper use and spelling of a word. It reflects not just on your general knowledge, but on your precision as well.

accept	grate	principal	their
except	great	principle	there
			they're
aisle	heard	profit	to
isle	herd	prophet	too
			two
bear	hour	rack	vain
bare	our	wrack	vane
			vein
berry	lead	rye	ware
bury	led	wry	wear
			where
cede	morning	seam	weather
seed	mourning	seem	whether
complement	oar	sight	
compliment	ore	site	
		cite	

crews	penance
cruise	pennants
discreet	pray
discrete	prey

Understanding the sense of a word helps us to both use it correctly and spell it properly. Consider *interment* and *internment*. Sometimes sloppy pronunciation makes these two words seem similar. However, their intended meanings in the sentence should be clear. Burying someone is an *interment;* detaining a person is an *internment*. This distinction is cheerfully brought to you by your dictionary!

The contraction *it's* and the possessive pronoun *its* (see p. 26) are other examples in which spelling depends on knowing the sense of words. In this case, good grammar requires us to know the difference between *it's* and *its,* but a knowledge of their meanings is a giant step toward avoiding errors in their selection.

STRUCTURE

Just as our language has rules dealing with agreement, case and punctuation, so too does it have rules that control spelling.

Although it may seem that spelling rules are riddled with exceptions, most words are covered by these guidelines. Let's examine several of the key rules—and deal gingerly with the exceptions.

Surviving suffixes

A *suffix* is a group of letters added to a root word to give it new or added meaning. For example, when you add *-ible* to *access,* you have *accessible,* which means "easy to approach." Sometimes, however, suffixes are tacked onto incomplete roots. Take *dispense:* If you want a suffix after it to denote "an ability to dispense," you would add *-able,* and because the last letter of the root is a vowel, you drop it and make *dispensable.* (As you might expect, the dropping of the vowel doesn't always occur.)

Why, you might ask, do we have *-ible* and *-able* when they mean the same thing? The answer has to do with the history of our language; *-ible* connects with Old Latin-based verbs, and *-able* has Old French and Anglo-Saxon lineage. The use of *-able* or *-ible* gives you a clue to the word's origin. However, you will find that *-able* words outnumber the *-ible* ones.

The other suffixes you should master are *-ance/-ant* and *-ence/-ent*. These, too, come from French and Latin, and the *-a* or *-e* choice has to do only with the original form of the Latin and the French word. Both *-ance* and *-ence* create nouns from verbs, indicating a state or quality as in *resistance* and *persistence*. Both *-ant* and *-ent* are used to form adjectives, as in *resistant* and *persistent*.

With this background, we can offer some general rules about the uses of these suffixes:

> **Not only is *-able* more common than *-ible*, but it also is used mostly with complete root words.**

Therefore, we have *workable, dependable* and *perishable*. Exceptions: A few root words drop their final *e* when adding *-able*. These include *desirable, excusable, indispensable* and *usable*. Fortunately, there aren't many of these! There are many more examples of the retention of the final *e*, such as *changeable* and *noticeable*.

> **Only *-able* follows *g, i* and the hard *c* ("k" sound).**

This dependable rule explains the spelling of *navigable, amiable* and *irrevocable*.

> **The suffix *-ible* is commonly used after double consonants (like *ll*), *s, st*, some *d* sounds and the soft *c* ("s" sound).**

This rule explains *infallible* and *horrible; divisible* and *plausible; edible* and *credible;* and *forcible* and *invincible*.

> **Sorry to say, but there are no firm rules for the use of *-ance/-ant* and *-ence/-ent* suffixes.**

However, here are some guidelines to help you make some distinctions:

- Their sounds. For example, *attendance* has an "ah" sound in its suffix, but *independence* has an "eh" sound.

- Your memory. Here are some of the more difficult ones to remember:

AN	EN
attendance	existence
descendant	independence
maintenance	persistent
relevant	recurrent
resistant	superintendent

Remember—you have only two choices with these words. When in doubt, look it up. It won't take that long.

IE-EI-OH!

The *ie/ei* dilemma is not overwhelming. These guidelines should help:

The *-ie* spelling is more common than *-ei*. And *i* usually precedes *e* unless it follows a *c* that carries an "s" sound.

Here are some examples:

Before or Without C	After C
fierce	deceit
hygiene	perceive
niece	receipt
wield	receive

Note that French *-ier* words like *financier* don't violate the *-ei* after *c* rule. The *-ier* just happens to be a standard ending.

It's more demanding to remember those *-ei* constructions:

- words with long "a" sounds, such as *weigh* and *freight*
- words with long "an" sounds, such as *feign* and *reign*
- five exceptions that just demand memorization: *caffeine, leisure, protein, seize* and *weird.*

If a *c* carries a "sh" sound, it probably will be followed by *ie.*

Examples include:

ancient   deficient   sufficient

To double or not to double the consonant

When you add *-ing* or *-ed* to a word, you generally double a final consonant only if:

- the word ends in a single consonant. So, *commit* becomes *committing* and *committed*.

- that consonant is preceded by a single vowel. *Commit* is safe here, so the final consonant can be doubled.

- the accent is placed on the last syllable. The pronunciation is *commit* (accented syllable underlined), so our rule is valid. Note these other examples, where all three guidelines are met:

  acquitted   equipping   occurring   omitted

Once you understand this rule, you can see that certain words will not double their final consonant. This occurs when:

- the accent is not on the final syllable of the root word. This explains *canceled* and *traveling*. Note their accents:

  cancel   travel

This also explains the spelling of *profited*.

- no vowel precedes the final consonant. This explains *investing*; a consonant precedes the final *t*.

Take note of one other guideline: The suffix *-ment* doesn't require doubling the final consonant of the root word. Because *-ment* begins with a consonant, there is no need to alter the root. So, we have *equipping* but *equipment*, *allotting* but *allotment*, *committed* but *commitment*.

That battalion of harassing and embarrassing words

Words of explanation almost fail when we discuss the next list of words. They are frustrating but not overwhelming. Although reliable rules seem to have been abandoned, sound can be a great help. Examining differences in pronunciations and meanings can help, too.

This list of troublesome word pairs and groups is not comprehensive, but it should help you in many cases:

accumulate	inoculate	religious
accommodate	innovative	sacrilegious
battalion	millionaire	theater
medallion	questionnaire	massacre
census	proceed	vilify
consensus	precede	villain
	supersede	
embarrass	recommend	
harass	occasional	

SOME FINAL WORDS

Here is a list of difficult spellings that vex many writers—some of the words most commonly misspelled by students and professionals. Notice that many of the guidelines and suggestions mentioned in this chapter can help you spell these words correctly.

Remember: *When in doubt, look it up! Above all, don't rely on your spell-checker!* Your credibility as a writer is at stake.

acceptable	accessible	accidentally	accommodate
accumulate	acknowledgment	acquit	adviser
a lot	annihilate	argument	athletic
bankruptcy	believe	bookkeeper	broccoli
business	caffeine	calendar	canceled
cemetery	changeable	commitment	comparable
condemn	conscious	consensus	courageous
criticize	definite	desirable	desperate
deterrent	dilemma	ecstasy	eighth
embarrass	excusable	exhilarate	existence
financier	forcible	harassment	hemorrhage
hygiene	indispensable	innocuous	inoculate
irascible	irresistible	jeopardy	judgment
legitimate	leisure	likable	likelihood
loneliness	manageable	millionaire	niece

noticeable	occasion	occurrence	omitted
parallel	permissible	persistent	potatoes
precede	predecessor	privilege	procedure
protein	questionnaire	recommend	relevant
repetitious	resistant	rhythm	seizure
separate	sheriff	skillful	sovereign
succeed	supersede	surprise	tariff
temperament	vacillate	vacuum	vilify
villain	weird	wield	willful
withhold	woolen	woolly	yield

CHAPTER 9

Clarity, Conciseness, Coherence

People who think clear, crisp writing flows "naturally" from the pens of good writers couldn't be more mistaken. Good writing is hard work, and the better you are—or want to be—the harder it is. Veteran writers labor over each choice of word, the creation of each clause, sentence and paragraph. They know that direct, powerful writing says precisely what the author means to say—no more, no less, no fuzziness, no confusion, no second or third reading necessary. They know that this kind of writing is the result of many decisions mindfully made. What am I trying to say? Is this what I mean? Is it precisely what I mean? Is this the very best way to say what I mean?

Writers who care about the quality of their work talk to themselves as they write, edit and revise, asking themselves the same questions, doggedly, word by word, sentence by sentence, paragraph by paragraph. If you are interested in producing clear, forceful prose, you need to start talking to yourself too!

Good writing is no accident. It is the result of good decisions. Some of these decisions appear to be mechanical only: spelling, vocabulary, grammar, punctuation. But clarity, conciseness and coherence underlie each choice.

CHOOSING WORDS

As we form ideas in our heads about what we want to say, we are immediately confronted with the most fundamental choice: the individual word. The words we choose must communicate precisely what we mean with a minimum of fuss and a maximum of power. This is particularly true with verbs, the engines of the sentence. Choosing the *correct* verb is a matter of grammar; choosing the *right* verb is a matter of conciseness and clarity.

AVOIDING *UP*

> She was chosen to <u>head up</u> the delegation.
>
> The president must <u>face up</u> to the crisis.
>
> The construction <u>slowed up (down)</u> traffic all morning.

None of these verbs needs the preposition *up*. All of them are weakened by the extra word. *Up* doesn't add meaning to these verbs; it takes away crispness. This may seem like a minor point, but it is at this basic level that good writing begins.

> She was chosen to <u>head</u> the delegation.
>
> The president must <u>face</u> the problem.
>
> The accident <u>slowed</u> traffic all morning.

Beware of *free up* (free), *wake up* (awake), *stand up* (stand) and *shake up* (shake). In these instances, *up* is more than unnecessary; it is sloppy.

Of course, some verbs need *up* to complete their meaning. *Make* does not mean the same thing as *make up*. *Break* is not synonymous with *break up*. *Up* is necessary for the meaning of *pick up*. In these cases, *up* is not clutter, but neither is it strong, precise writing.

> He accused the senator of <u>making up</u> the allegations. (weak)
>
> He accused the senator of <u>fabricating</u> the allegations. (stronger)
>
> The investigation <u>broke up</u> the crime syndicate. (weak)
>
> The investigation <u>shattered</u> the crime syndicate. (stronger)
>
> The economy is <u>picking up</u>. (weak)
>
> The economy is <u>recovering</u>. (stronger)

"VERBIZING" NOUNS

> The committee must <u>prioritize</u> its concerns, <u>concretize</u> its goals, <u>definitize</u> its objectives and <u>operationalize</u> its plan before it <u>fractionalizes</u> the community and <u>destabilizes</u> its natural constituency.

The suffix -*ize* is on the loose, "verbizing" and "uglyizing" our language. Some people think you can tack -*ize* on to any noun and create a verb. Many of those makeshift verbs are unnecessary. *Fractionalize*, for example, means nothing more than *split*. Other words with longer linguistic histories, like *utilize* and *signalize*, serve no distinct purpose. *Utilize* has come to mean nothing more than *use*. *Signalize* means *signal*. Not only are many of these -*ize* words useless, but they are also grating to the ear, long-winded and stuffy.

Of course, yesterday's awkward jargon is today's respectable word. *Pasteurize* must have raised the hackles of 19th-century grammarians, but few would be upset about it today. It is difficult to say how many of the newly created, tongue-twisting -*ize* verbs will become permanent additions to our language. (The fewer the better, we think.) While we are all awaiting the verdict, we can subject an awkward-sounding -*ize* verb to three tests:

1. Is it listed in the dictionary as an acceptable (not informal, colloquial or slang) word?

2. Does it have a unique meaning?

3. Does it have a sound that is, at the very least, not displeasing?

If the word passes the three tests, use it. If it fails, find another word. Do not "jargonize" and "awkwardize" the language. It may be all right to *pasteurize* milk, but it is not yet acceptable to *zucchinize* a casserole.

THAT

That performs several grammatical functions. It is an adjective:

> <u>That</u> book won the Pulitzer prize.
> (*That* describes *book*.)

It is a demonstrative pronoun:

<u>That</u> will get you in trouble.
(*That* takes the place of a noun.)

It is a relative pronoun:

This is an invention <u>that</u> could make millions.
(*That* introduces a relative clause.)

It is a conjunction:

The researchers admitted <u>that</u> they falsified data.
(*That* links two independent clauses.)

The troublesome uses of *that* are as a conjunction and as a relative pronoun. Simply put, writers overuse the word. *That* is often unnecessary in a sentence. Its inclusion slows the pace of the sentence and often robs the sentence of its grace and rhythm. If a word does not add meaning, get rid of it. Consider these sentences, all of which would be crisper without *that:*

The researchers admitted ~~that~~ they falsified data.

Government sources say ~~that~~ the study is flawed.

The statement ~~that~~ the senator made infuriated the committee.

Often all you need to do is remove the useless *that*. However, some sentences demand revision. Conciseness is the issue.

Police recovered the limousine <u>that was stolen</u>. (wordy)

Police recovered the <u>stolen</u> limousine. (improved)

The photograph <u>that she took</u> won first prize. (wordy)

<u>Her</u> photograph won first prize. (improved)

That is sometimes used legitimately to link sentence parts. To discover whether *that* is necessary to a sentence, ask yourself two questions:

1. Can *that* be eliminated with no change in the meaning of the sentence?

2. Can the clause introduced by *that* be expressed more concisely?

If you answer *yes* to either question, edit or rewrite.

REDUNDANCY AND WORDINESS

In the old days, newspaper reporters and authors got paid by the word (some freelance magazine writers still do). Light-hearted criticism of the beloved—but wordy—novels of Charles Dickens makes a point of this 18th- and 19th-century practice. Dickens was paid by the word, so he wrote lots of them, say some of those who lose patience with the author's long-windedness. The fatter the book, the fatter the paycheck.

Today, in our world of instantaneous communication, e-mails, faxes and 10-second sound bites, we think quite differently about excess verbiage. "Write as if you had to pay for every word," a college teacher once counseled his journalism students. One of those students, who later became a journalism professor himself, offered the same advice to his students, but with a twist. He recorded commercials during the Super Bowl (the most expensive commercial time on television), divided the cost of the airwaves by the number of words and found that in some commercials each word cost $13,000. Talk is decidedly not cheap. Make your words count.

Ignorance of the real meanings of words, attempts at false erudition, repetition of other people's jargon, murky thinking and sheer sloppiness all result in the writer falling prey to wordiness and redundancy. Consider these examples:

mutual cooperation
(*Cooperation* means "acting for mutual benefit." *Mutual* is redundant.)

end result
(*Result*, by definition, is the end consequence.)

very unique
(*Unique* is one of a kind. It either is or isn't.)

incumbent officeholder
(The definition of *incumbent* is officeholder.)

consensus of opinion
(*Consensus* means "collective opinion.")

repeat again
(*Repeat* includes *again* within its definition.)

refer back
(*Refer* includes *back* in its definition.)

more universal

more universally accepted
(*Universal* means "worldwide." How can it be more than worldwide?)

Other wordy, sluggish expressions have crept into writing. Here are some of the more common ones to avoid:

Avoid	Use Instead
as of now	now
at the present time	now
at this point in time	now
despite the fact that	although
due to the fact that	because
on account of	because
seeing as how	because
during the course of	during

VAGUE WORDS

When we speak, thinking as we talk, sometimes searching for words or fumbling with thoughts, we often insert such meaningless vagaries as *a type of*, *a kind of* or *in terms of*. You might hear yourself say something like this one day: "It was the type of thing I was kind of proud of, I mean in terms of personal accomplishments." Huh? That's bad enough in speech. It is absolutely inadmissible in writing. The solution: Think before you write. Edit, edit, edit.

Years of writing term papers and hearing equivocal bureaucratic language have cemented in our minds such filler words as *aspect, element, factor, situation, character, condition*.

The aspect of the situation that will be a factor will depend on the character of the elements we must contend with.

These are the words you use when you don't know what you're talking about. The result is not only the opposite of clear writing; it is the opposite of any communication. Should these words crop up in your prose, weed them out mercilessly.

EUPHEMISMS AND "FANCY WORDS"

When people or organizations want to protect themselves or hide bad news or soften potentially offensive information, they create *euphemisms*—generally vague, often purposefully misleading, but inoffensive, ways of saying (or not saying) what they mean. When the Internal Revenue Service finally stopped pursuing a taxpayer who had, in fact, done nothing wrong, the agency sent this note:

> The audit issue was reconsidered and determined not to have existed.

Audit issue is sanitized code for a fierce, three-year battle between the taxpayer and the agency. *Reconsidered,* in this case, means the IRS finally figured out it was wrong. Note how skillfully this eerie sentence substitutes euphemism for a clear expression—*we made a mistake.* The sentence is carefully constructed to obscure an admission of error.

Euphemisms are all around us. A company, deeply in debt, might announce to its stockholders that it is "currently experiencing a budgetary shortfall." Another, found guilty of dumping toxic waste in a river, might admit that its "compliance statistics showed a downturn." The military wins the prize for creating both the most and the most chilling euphemisms. "Entry into a nonpermissive environment" was the military's way of evading the word *invasion* when U.S. troops were poised to enter Haiti. *Friendly fire* softens the terrible tragedy of the action it describes: gunfire against troops by their own troops. *Collateral damage* is a euphemism for killing civilians.

Let's say it's snowing outside with a wind chill factor of 10 below zero, and you look out the window and see a man running down the street dressed only in a bathing suit. What would you be most likely to say? What would clearly, precisely and directly express the moment? "Look at that guy! He must be nuts!" A master of euphemism would see the same thing and quietly comment that the man was "somewhat inappropriately attired given the climatic conditions." Writers can't stop others from manufacturing euphemisms, but they can refuse to transmit them.

A related clarity problem is "fancy words." We don't mean three-dollar words like *prestidigitation* or *ovolactovegetarianism.* We mean silly, inflated words that take the place of good, plain, ordinary, serviceable words: *vehicle* for car (or truck), *facility* for building, *infrastructure* for roads and bridges, *domicile* for home. Stay clear of these pretensions. If others use them, your responsibility as a public communicator is to not pass them on.

JARGON

The first meaning of the word *jargon*, one dictionary tells us, is "the inarticulate utterances of birds; meaningless chatter." Of course, the word more commonly means the specialized language of a trade or profession. But as writers we ought to take to heart that first definition. To our audience, jargon is, more often than not, meaningless chatter.

Scientific, technical and scholarly diction insulates members of a profession from the outside world, excluding "nonmembers" from what is being said. "Members" may talk or write to one another in jargon, using it as shorthand or code. That's one thing. But *public* communicators—media writers—have a responsibility to communicate clearly and simply to wider audiences. Writers should be jargon slayers, not jargon purveyors.

Here is a scientist deep in the throes of jargon:

Despite rigid re-examination of all experimental variables, this protocol continued to produce data at variance with our subsequently proven hypothesis.
(translation: The experiment didn't work.)

Here is cop talk:

While doing OPs to watch a set, we raised the player and he beelined.
(translation: During observation of a drug deal, the dealer got wind of the cops and beat it.)

Jargon can be used to obscure ideas or make ordinary ideas sound more important. It can also be used to hide meaning or desensitize people to issues. For a writer to perpetuate such jargon signals a profound failure to communicate. Consider this sampling of military jargon:

During today's <u>sorties</u>, coalition forces <u>visited</u> and <u>acquired</u> 40 sites. <u>Incontinent</u> <u>ordnance</u> was reported to have caused considerable <u>collateral damage</u>.
(translation: The military bombed and destroyed 40 targets. Bombing errors killed a number of civilians.)

Although jargon serves a purpose for those within a profession, it serves no purpose in public writing. Using jargon does not make you sound impressive. On the contrary, you impress (and help) your audience by lucidly explaining difficult material, not repeating words and phrases you do not understand.

PUTTING WORDS TOGETHER

Clear, concise, coherent writing depends on more than careful word choice. Proper placement of words is also imperative. Misplacement mistakes can easily harm the clarity of your prose.

MISPLACED WORDS

In a sentence, a modifier needs to point directly and clearly to what it modifies. This generally means placing the modifier next to or as close as possible to what it is modifying. Adverbs like *only, nearly, almost, just, scarcely, even, hardly* and *merely* create the biggest potential difficulty because their placement can drastically change the meaning of the sentence. Note how placement changes meaning in the following sentences:

Only she can explain it to you.
(No one else can explain it.)

She can only explain it to you.
(She can't do anything more than explain it to you.)

She can explain it to only you.
(She can't explain it to anyone else.)

Notice how the placement of *almost* in the next two sentences changes the meaning:

Negotiations almost broke down on every clause in the contract.
(Negotiations did not quite break down.)

Negotiations broke down on almost every clause in the contract.
(Just about every clause caused problems during negotiations.)

When we speak, we often have a devil-may-care attitude toward the placement of adverbs. But, because placement most surely and definitely changes meaning, stick to the old rule: Place the adverb (or other word) next to or as close as possible to the word you intend it to modify.

MISPLACED PHRASES AND CLAUSES

Like individual words, phrases and clauses should be placed next to or near what they modify. Again, placement affects meaning, as these examples illustrate:

> Hundreds of farms were devastated by flash floods <u>across the Midwest</u>.
>
> Hundreds of farms <u>across the Midwest</u> were devastated by flash floods.

Note how the phrase *across the Midwest* in the first sentence modifies *floods*. The meaning here is that the entire Midwest region suffered flash floods. In the second sentence, we do not know how large an area was affected by the flooding. We do know that Midwestern farms were hurt.

> The plan <u>that the student council is debating</u> will alter the university's free speech policy.
>
> The plan will alter the university's free speech policy <u>that the student council is debating</u>.

In the first sentence, the *plan* is being debated. In the second example, the *policy* is being debated.

DANGLING MODIFIERS

A modifier "dangles" when what it is supposed to modify is not part of the sentence. For example:

> To be successful in this business, perseverance is needed.

The phrase *to be successful in this business* does not modify anything in the sentence. The only word it could modify is *perseverance*, but that makes no sense. *Perseverance* is not trying to be successful in this business. The sentence needs to be revised:

> To be successful in this business, you must persevere.

Now the phrase correctly modifies *you*. Not only that, the revised sentence is in the active voice. The dangling modifier sentence was in the passive voice. Here is another dangling modifier:

> After studying for more than three years, Spanish came easily to him.

Clearly, *Spanish* did not study for more than three years; *he* did the studying. The sentence needs to be reconstructed so the introductory phrase clearly modifies the correct word. Coherence is at stake here.

> After studying for more than three years, he found Spanish was easy to master.

SPLIT CONSTRUCTIONS

Just as modifiers need to rest closely to what they modify, so other parts of the sentence must be placed carefully to maintain clarity and coherence of thought.

Split verbs often lead to incoherence. In most cases, it is best to keep auxiliary verbs next to the main verb and to avoid splitting infinitives. Consider what happens to sentence unity and graceful expression when you separate auxiliary verbs from the main verb:

> Refugees <u>have been</u> for more than three months <u>living</u> in temporary camps near the border. (auxiliary and main verb split)

> For more than three months, refugees <u>have been living</u> in temporary camps near the border. (improved)

The more words you place between the verb parts, the less coherent the sentence becomes. Occasionally, however, it is acceptable— even preferable—to split a multipart verb. Almost always, the verb is split by a single word, an adverb:

> Noise <u>has</u> always <u>been</u> a problem in the apartment complex.

Placing *always* between the verb parts does not hinder coherence. In fact, it adds emphasis.

Infinitives (*to be* forms of the verb) should also, in most cases, remain intact. Split infinitives contribute to awkwardness and interfere with coherent thought. A sentence should read smoothly and make sense.

City officials promised <u>to</u> as soon as possible <u>look</u> into the noise problem. (split infinitive)

City officials promised <u>to look</u> into the noise problem as soon as possible. (improved)

To aid sentence clarity and to help readers or listeners understand quickly what you are trying to say, keep the subject and the verb as close as possible. Look at what happens to coherence when subject and verb are interrupted by lengthy explanatory material:

The <u>agency</u>, following weeks of internal debate that resulted in the
(subj.)

reshuffling of hundreds of employees, <u>restructured</u> two of its bureaus.
(verb)

The sentence forces readers or listeners to wade through 14 words between the subject (*agency*) and its verb (*restructured*). But readers may have neither the time nor the inclination to slog through such constructions, and listeners can easily lose the thread of meaning. Be kind to your audience. Keep subject and verb close:

The <u>agency</u> <u>restructured</u> two of its bureaus following weeks of
(subj.)   (verb)

internal debate that resulted in the reshuffling of hundreds of employees.

Consider one more common splitting problem: a verb and its complements. The simplest construction to understand is subject-verb-object. It answers the basic question: "Who did what to whom?" Just as splitting the subject (*who*) from the verb (*did what*) interferes with clarity and coherence, so too does splitting the verb (*did what*) from its complement (*to whom*). Keep the verb and its complements (object, adverb, descriptive phrase) as close together as possible. You will promote sentence unity, readability and coherence.

Consumer advocates <u>protested</u> yesterday morning in front of
(verb)

several local toy stores <u>what they say is the marketing of violence to children through the sale of toy guns</u>. (complement)

This sentence makes readers or listeners wait nine words until they discover what the consumer advocates were upset about. The sentence is also clumsy. To avoid losing coherent thought—and your audience—rewrite:

> Consumer advocates protested what they say is the marketing of violence to children through the sale of toy guns. Marching (picketing, assembling, gathering) in front of several local toy stores yesterday morning, they . . .

MAKING SENSE

Every good grammatical decision you make contributes to clarity, conciseness and coherence. Choosing strong, precise words is the first step. Placing these words correctly is the next. Focusing on the architecture of sentences is the third level.

PARALLEL STRUCTURE

When you place like ideas in like grammatical patterns, you create *parallel structure*. As we discussed in Chapter 4, parallel structure aligns related ideas and presents them through the repetition of grammatical structure. It is vital to both clarity and unity, and it helps create rhythm and grace in a sentence. To create parallel structure using single words, you use a series of words that are the same part of speech. For example:

> This newest IRS ruling is preposterous, incomprehensible and illegal.

The related ideas are the criticisms of the IRS ruling. The grammatical pattern is the repetition of single adjectives.

To create parallel structure using phrases or clauses, replicate the grammatical pattern:

> Meditating can clear your mind, relax your body and enliven your spirit. (repeating phrases)

> If you sit correctly, if you breath deeply, if you quiet your mind, you can reach enlightenment. (repeating clauses)

Parallel structure binds ideas and enhances your audience's understanding of each idea by creating a lucid pattern. If you begin a sentence by establishing a particular grammatical pattern and then break the implicit contract you have made with your audience, you create confusion and disharmony.

Parallel structure is commonly used to introduce complementary, contrasting or sequential ideas. The relationship between the ideas can be implicit (as in the examples offered thus far), or it can be made apparent by using signal words. For example:

> Complementary relationship: *both/and, not only/but also*
>
> Contrasting relationship: *either/or, neither/nor*
>
> Sequential relationship: *first/second/third*
>
> <u>Both</u> the construction of bike lanes <u>and</u> the rerouting of delivery trucks should ease traffic in the university district.
> (complementary relationship, parallel structure)
>
> <u>Either</u> we enforce the clean air standards <u>or</u> we all buy gas masks.
> (contrasting relationship, parallel structure)
>
> <u>First</u>, define the problem; <u>second</u>, gather the information; <u>third</u>, brainstorm the alternatives.
> (sequential relationship, parallel structure)

Whether you make the relationship explicit by using signal words or implicit by letting the ideas speak for themselves, parallel structure is vital to clarity and coherence.

SENTENCE FRAGMENTS

As you remember from Chapter 3, a fragment is a group of words that lacks a subject, a predicate, a complete thought or any combination of the three. Grammatically, a fragment cannot stand alone. When readers see a group of words beginning with a capital letter and ending with a period, they expect a complete sentence. If instead you offer them a fragment, you confuse them. Unintentional fragments hinder both coherence and clarity.

> Computers have revolutionized information gathering. <u>Although they have their drawbacks</u>. (fragment underlined)

This fragment obscures meaning and clarity. Perhaps the writer meant:

Although they have their drawbacks, computers have revolutionized information gathering.

Maybe the writer meant no such connection. Perhaps the fragment was meant to signal the beginning of a new idea:

Computers have revolutionized information gathering. Although they have their drawbacks, their speed and efficiency are unrivaled.

Fragments leave your audience hanging, forcing them to guess your intended meaning. Offer your audience clear, complete thoughts. Fragments used knowingly, sparingly and stylistically are another story. See Chapter 10 to find out more about this.

RUN-ON SENTENCES

A run-on sentence is composed of two, three or any number of whole, complete sentences. Chapter 3 discussed the run-on as a grammatical problem. Here we want to emphasize it as an obstacle to concise and coherent writing.

The two most common run-on sentences are those inappropriately linked with *and* and those incorrectly spliced with commas. Both can confuse and frustrate a reader.

The university must deal with a shrinking budget and class sizes will increase. (run-on)

When you use *and* to link two independent clauses as in this example, you are saying that the two thoughts reinforce or directly complement each other or follow one another sequentially. If this isn't the case, as in the preceding example, you have created not just a run-on but also an incoherent sentence. If the thoughts in the clauses are not related in a definable, explicit way, rewrite the run-on as two separate sentences. If the thoughts are related, use a connecting word to signal the correct relationship.

Because the university must deal with a shrinking budget, class sizes will increase. (improved)

Note that the run-on was corrected by subordinating one thought (clause) to another to clarify and make explicit the relationship between the two clauses.

When commas link clauses, readers expect the words following a comma to add to or complement what they have just read. If the clauses are not related in this way, the result is an incoherent run-on.

> The legislature mandated cutbacks throughout the university, class sizes increased dramatically, class offerings decreased significantly.

This run-on sentence needs to be rewritten with the relationship between the clauses clearly expressed. Commas are the wrong signal here. In the absence of correct signals, it is unclear exactly what relationship exists.

> <u>Soon after</u> the legislature mandated cutbacks throughout the university, class size increased dramatically, <u>and</u> class offerings decreased significantly.

Now the relationship between the three thoughts is clear.

CLARITY, CONCISENESS, COHERENCE

Writers write to be understood. Whether they are writing to inform, amuse, uplift, persuade or cajole, their thoughts must be clear; their sentences must be comprehensible. Clarity, conciseness and coherence begin with individual word choice. From that point on, every grammatical decision either enhances or detracts from this triple goal. Imprecision, clutter, misplaced phrases and murky construction have no place in good writing. The goal is lean, powerful communication. It is not an easy goal. But it is—with practice, patience, hard work and a firm grasp of grammar—an attainable one.

CHAPTER 10

Style

There's competence, and then there's excellence. There are stories you read because the subject is of particular interest to you: the storm approaching your area, an upcoming concert by one of your favorite groups, guns confiscated at the local high school. Then there are stories you read because the writing is so good, so compelling, that you find yourself reading about Tupperware or the Dalai Lama or environmental allergies not because you were already interested but because the writer *made* you interested.

How do writers do that? How do writers move from correctness, clarity and competence to something more—to stylish, graceful, compelling writing? There is no easy answer here. This is, after all, a writer's life work, the evolution of craft. Excellence doesn't just happen. It is carefully, thoughtfully, imaginatively and patiently built. Are you ready to begin building?

WHAT IS STYLE?

Style is an integral component of writing that reflects the writer's way of seeing, thinking and using language. It is the writer's unique vision—and the lively, original expression of that vision—that draws audience attention to the message. It is the product of purposeful choices, the culmination of many small things done well, the result of sheer hard work. It is not just the private domain of novelists and poets. Style has an important place in all writing.

Novice writers, and many experienced ones as well, harbor several dangerous misconceptions about style:

- They believe if they write clean, clutterless prose, their writing will lack style.

- They believe style is like a garnish, a spicy condiment added to bring zip to bland writing. They believe style has something to do with ornamentation or flashiness.

- They fear that style, because it is hard to define ("I don't know what it is, but I know it when I see it"), is therefore mysterious and unattainable.

They are wrong on all counts.

As any stylish writer will tell you, style emerges from—and cannot exist without—crisp, lean, language use. First come the fundamentals: strong verbs, grammatical consistency, tightly constructed sentences. Then comes style. Novelist John Updike looks at style by comparing the process of writing to the process of becoming a musician. Musicians begin by learning to identify and play individual notes. They learn how to read music. They practice scales. They play simple compositions. Only after mastering these fundamentals can they begin to develop their own manner of musical expression, their own style. Writers too must master the basics before they can find their own "voice."

Writer William Zinsser likes to think of writers as carpenters. First writers must learn to "saw wood neatly" and "drive nails." Later they can "bevel the edges." A beveled edge (style) is pretty, but if the structure isn't built right (constructed grammatically) it will collapse.

Writers as musicians, writers as carpenters—the message is clear: First, learn the *craft* of writing; then explore the *art*. Precise grammatical language (lean, clutterless prose) does not stand in the way of stylish writing. On the contrary, it is the *basis* for stylish writing.

Style, then, has little to do with ostentatious language. Window dressing (a clutter of adjectives, for example), verbal ornamentation (big words or "purple prose") and fancy tricks do not generally contribute to stylish writing. In fact, verbal flashiness can obscure coherent thought. There is nothing flashy, but everything stylish, about these first two paragraphs of Carrie Dolan's *Wall Street Journal* story:

> Out on an open range, a 1300-pound bull with ropes looped around his middle stands drooling in the dust. He is stubbornly

resisting efforts to load him into a stock trailer so he can be taken to the corral for medical treatment.

Jane Glennie gets out of her truck. She spits into her hand and grinds a glowing cigarette butt into her palm. While two mounted cowboys hold the ropes tight, she plants her boot on the bull's horn and shoves. The beast just jerks his head, drools and digs his hoofs deeper into the dirt. Mrs. Glennie grabs a shovel. A couple of hefty whacks later, the bull plods into a livestock trailer.

This is crisp, clean writing: simple sentences, strong verbs, powerful images. This is style.

The final misconception, that style is mysterious and unattainable, is the hardest to attack. Because it is unique to the individual writer, style does seem to defy definition. But that doesn't mean it's mysterious. It means it's personal, idiosyncratic and distinctive. Far from being mysterious, style is the sum of a series of good, solid decisions—many of them as basic as word choice or sentence construction—that a writer is aware enough, smart enough and experienced enough to make throughout the piece.

Style begins with accuracy and correctness and moves on to lively, original use of the language. It is always appropriate to the subject, the audience and the medium. Ultimately, it is the difference between a competent story and a memorable one.

Let's demystify style by examining some of its key components: liveliness, originality, rhythm and sound, and imagery.

LIVELINESS

Lively writing is not excitable, overwrought, exclamation-point-studded prose, but writing that moves along at a good clip, involving readers or listeners and carrying them briskly from paragraph to paragraph. Like all components of style, liveliness depends not only on the way you use the language but also on what you have to say.

In media writing, style and substance go hand in hand. Your skills as an observer, interviewer and information gatherer net the raw material. Your skill as a writer transforms that material into vibrant prose. So, how can you make your writing lively?

CHOOSE VERBS CAREFULLY

Strong, precise verbs give energy to a sentence; weak, vague or over-modified verbs sap a sentence of its power. Instead of tacking on adverbs to clarify the meaning of a verb, spend time searching for the one right word.

instead of <u>look at carefully</u>:   <u>examine, scrutinize</u>

instead of <u>think deeply</u>:   <u>ponder, deliberate</u>

instead of <u>walk unevenly</u>:   <u>lurch, stumble, stagger</u>

instead of <u>eat quickly</u>:   <u>gobble, wolf</u>

Note the simple, carefully chosen verbs in the lead sentence of this *Washington Post* story about a wrestler:

Six hundred pounds of Haystacks Calhoun <u>rises</u> to its full height of 6 feet 4 inches, <u>lumbers</u> outside his hotel on downtown H Street and <u>blocks out</u> the afternoon sun.

USE INTENSIFIERS SPARINGLY

The adverbs *very, really, truly, completely, extremely, positively, absolutely* and *so* often add nothing but clutter. They show sloppiness of thought and generally add a too-colloquial tone to writing. Instead of intensifying a weak word, search for a strong, precise one.

instead of <u>very funny</u>:   <u>hilarious</u>

instead of <u>extremely hungry</u>:   <u>ravenous</u>

instead of <u>really eager</u>:   <u>avid</u>

instead of <u>positively awful</u>:   <u>dreadful</u>

When you've found a strong word, leave it alone. Don't rob it of its impact by unnecessarily intensifying it.

really exhausted

extremely sweltering

truly exceptional

AVOID REDUNDANCIES

Understand the meanings of words before you use them. *More equal, more parallel* and *most unique* are redundant expressions you can easily avoid if you pay attention to the meanings of *equal, parallel* and *unique.*

EDIT TO REMOVE WORDINESS

Nothing destroys the vitality of prose faster, or as completely, as verbosity, clutter, "purple prose," or bureaucratese. Each word, each phrase, each clause, each sentence should survive a rigorous editing process because it adds meaning, substance or color to the piece. Making every word count is the challenge. Review "Redundancy and Wordiness," "Vague Words," "Euphemisms and Fancy Words" and "Jargon" in Chapter 9.

USE ACTIVE VOICE

As we've written in Chapter 6, active voice contributes to sharp, clear, vigorous sentence construction. In an active voice sentence, the actor performs the action. In a passive voice sentence, the actor has the action performed on it. Passive voice construction almost always weakens the verb and adds unnecessary words. It often sounds stilted and formal.

USE PRESENT TENSE

Present tense often allows the reader or listener to experience the story as it unfolds. When you use present tense as an element of style, you create a scene the audience can feel close to and involved with. There is an urgency and immediacy to the present tense that can enliven your writing. Consider this scene, recounted in present tense, from a longer piece about a tough-minded women's basketball coach:

> The assistant trainer <u>runs</u> over with a towel and ice, but the coach <u>keeps</u> her distance. She barely <u>looks</u> at Sandie. People get hurt in practice all the time. The coach <u>has</u> a sixth sense about whether it's serious or not. This one isn't. She doesn't <u>say</u> anything, but she <u>thinks</u> this minor injury has opened a little crack in Sandie, and her frustration about her poor playing, her anger with herself, is seeping out. She's lying there too long; she's wallowing in it, <u>thinks</u> the coach.

"Get her off the court or get a stretcher!" she <u>yells</u>, exasperated, from the sidelines.

Of course, the scene took place in the past. The writer is recounting it for the audience much later. But the present tense makes us feel as if we are there, courtside, watching the practice. The scene is alive. Of course, not all stories can or should be told in present tense. Often past or future tenses are essential for historical accuracy. But the technique of narrowing the gap between audience and story by using present tense has many applications. Scene setting is certainly one of them.

Another is *attribution.* Using present tense to attribute quotations or present dialogue in a story shows the immediacy of the comments, quickens the pace of the story and, in the case of conversational debate or opposing comments, shows the ongoing nature of the controversy. If a person said something yesterday, he or she would be likely to say the same thing today (unless, of course, we're talking about politicians).

No single element ensures lively writing. But if you use strong, precise language, rid your prose of clutter, stick with the active voice and use, where appropriate, the present tense, your writing will be crisper, snappier and more inviting.

ORIGINALITY

Originality of style cannot be separated from originality of substance. If, as a thinker, observer, interviewer and cultural forager, you gather fresh material and come to novel insights, then the written work you produce can be distinctive and original. When Health magazine columnist Mary Roach visited Florida to write about, of all things, Tupperware, she began her story this way:

The Tupperware World Headquarters in Orlando, Florida, is a collection of long, low modular buildings, the sort of shapes you could easily stack one on top of another for just-right storage in your pantry, fridge or freezer, if that's the sort of person you were.

The playful tone and the unique visual image create an unusually enticing first sentence. This is what originality is all about: a novel vision translated into simple but imaginative language. This is style.

Or consider this wonderful sentence in the middle of a National Public Radio story about the emergency room of an animal hospital:

> In the examination room to the right of Dr. Cabe, a rust-colored dog is lying very still on the mirror steel table, its four legs splaying out at odd angles over the counter, as the couple who owns him hold one another, their faces colorless and almost round from crying.

The writing here is spare; the description seems detached, almost clinical. This is on purpose. This is style. The writer could have described the dog owners' faces as "pale and swollen from crying." But that's a standard description. We've heard it in many different forms, too many times to be affected by it. But faces "colorless and almost round from crying"—that's original, fresh and affecting. We'll talk more about description and scene setting in the "Show, Don't Tell" section toward the end of this chapter. Let's concentrate now on originality of expression and on using language in fresh, vigorous ways.

AVOID CLICHÉS

A *cliché*, by definition, lacks originality. It is a trite or overused expression or idea. It's the image or the phrase that springs immediately to mind. We've heard it before; we've read it before. It is someone else's idea, and the more it is used, the less power it has. As author Donald Hall writes, "When we put words together . . . we begin to show our original selves, or we show a dull copy of someone else's original." Note the following cliché-ridden remark from an economist offering the year's forecast. Unfortunately for the economist, the remark was quoted extensively in the national media!

> Let's remember we climbed up the hill pretty darned quickly. We've had the rug pulled out from under us, but we've picked ourselves up, and maybe we can see the light at the end of the tunnel.

So, as the sun sinks slowly in the west, we bid a fond farewell to the tried and true expressions that creep into writing like a thief in the night, robbing it blind of its power.

Had enough? We could go on forever. Clichés take no more time to think of than they do to pound out on a keyboard. Creating original expressions, on the other hand, is hard work; it challenges your imaginative and linguistic powers.

PLAY WITH FIGURES OF SPEECH

Consider this simple but evocative simile in a *New York Times* story about a "spammer":

> Damien Melle, who makes a living sending huge amounts of e-mail advertising over the Internet, works out of his home in this hardscrabble Southern California suburb, in an office where the smell of fried food lingers like, say, unwanted e-mail in your in box.

Or how about this metaphor in the middle of a quirky feature about a man who collects antique toasters and opened a toaster museum:

> Ten years ago, Norcross' toaster obsession was unshaped dough on the breadboard of his life.

These writers are having fun. What grabs us when we read these two sentences, what makes us smile, is the unique vision, the odd or wonderfully apt comparisons. *Similes* are verbal comparison that use *like* or *as* to announce themselves. Original similes have power, impact, even humor. Run-of-the-mill comparisons or clichés contribute nothing: *as black as night, as cool as a cucumber, hair like spun gold.* These comparisons lack verve and originality. Where is the imaginative stretch in *as black as night*? Night *is* black. What's the interesting comparison here? There is none.

Whereas similes are explicit comparisons using *like* or *as,* *metaphors* express a more direct comparison. Instead of stating that item A is *like* item B (a simile), a metaphor states that item A *is* item B. In the preceding example, the toaster collector's obsession was not *like* unshaped dough, it *was* unshaped dough.

When you attribute human characteristics, feelings or behaviors to nonhuman or inanimate objects, you are using a device called *personification.* Rushing to meet a deadline, you see the clock "staring" down at you. Clocks don't actually stare, of course. You've attributed a human quality to a mechanical object. You've personified the clock (albeit with a cliché!). Here, newspaper and magazine writer Jeff Stoffer personifies a mountain range:

> The county's most dramatic geologic formation, the rugged and sprawling thirty-mile-long Steens Mountain . . . is the highest exposed geologic fault in North America, its shoulders tattered with 2-million-year-old glaciation scars.

If you are thinking to yourself, "Figures of speech are fine for poets and authors, but I'm a journalist," think again. As the examples in this section show, writers of all persuasions can and do use literary devices to add zest to their writing. As information consumers become increasingly inundated by media messages, it becomes even more important to craft your message—be it a news story or advertising copy—in original and memorable ways, like using similes, metaphors and personification.

PLAY WITH WORDS

As we prepare to wash our hands of the 20th century, America's gone germ crazy.

The makers of Dial soap are in a lather over a magazine ad for a liquid cleanser that showed disease-causing micro-organisms superimposed over a picture of a soap bar.

Non-smokers celebrated clean air in restaurants Friday, but smokers fumed as a no-smoking law they perceive as a breach of civil rights took effect.

These sentences, taken from news and magazine stories, show original language use. In the first, the cliché "washing one's hands of . . . ," meaning being done with something, gets new life when used literally in a story about antibacterial soaps. In the second, the word *lather* plays on a double meaning—lather as soap foam and lather as "in a lather" (agitated). In the third sentence, the word *fumed* transforms an ordinary sentence into a story opener with a bit of zip. All these plays on words are simple, straightforward, appropriate to the subject—and fun.

But playful language need not be limited to lighthearted treatment of material. Consider this lead sentence by a science journalist writing a serious profile of a DNA researcher:

He's high on the scientists' favorite drug—discovery.

Word play need not be complicated or devastatingly witty to be effective. It need only be original, memorable and, of course, appropriate to the tone of the message.

RHYTHM AND SOUND

Words march to a beat. Long sentences move gently, liltingly, picking up momentum as they flow. Short sentences create a staccato beat. Repetition of words or phrases can add accent and meter. In short, sentence construction communicates. Words may have power, but words set in rhythmic sentences have clout. Let's examine five components of rhythmic sentence construction: repetition, parallelism, sentence length, fragments and run-ons.

USE REPETITION

Purposeful repetition of words or phrases can be used to add rhythm and grace to sentences. But, like all stylistic devices, it should be used sparingly. Too much repetition leads to boredom and clunkiness.

In the following magazine story lead, note the repetition of *it/it's:*

It looks like silt, smells like Lake Erie on a bad day, tastes like week-old cod and costs almost $3 an ounce. And everyone's buying it.

"It's the most potent food on earth," claims one devotee turned distributor.

"It's another gimmick to rip people off," insists a local physician.

It's spirulina maxima, a spiral-shaped blue-green alga.

Repetition of a single word performs three stylistic functions here: It quickens the pace of the story by establishing a rhythm that pulls the reader from paragraph to paragraph; it creates smooth transitions from paragraph to paragraph; it sets up a mystery (What is "it"?) that presumably the reader will want to solve.

In tapping out a meter, repetition creates emphasis. The word or phrase you repeat assumes prominence and becomes a focal point. In the following passage, repetition of the word *gray* makes the point rhythmically and emphatically:

At 5:30 on a December morning in Oregon you have to dig deep just to make it out of bed. About the best you can hope for this time of year is a slate gray dawn that lightens to a dove gray morning that slips into a pearl gray afternoon.

Can you feel the rhythmic insistence of the word *gray* and the clear (if dreary) meaning it conveys? Repetition can be a powerful, dramatic and compelling technique. Perhaps that's why it is a favorite of speech writers who want to add drama and force to the spoken word. Some of the most remembered and most quoted public speeches depend on the element of repetition: Winston Churchill's compelling "We shall fight on the beaches . . ." World War II speech, which used the "We shall fight" litany to pound out both a rhythm and a message; John F. Kennedy's "Let them come to Berlin" speech that repeated this sentence with increasing force.

CREATE POWER WITH PARALLELISM

Parallelism is actually a kind of repetition, the repetition of grammatical patterns used to convey parallel or similar ideas. Parallelism is thus simultaneously a component of agreement (Chapter 4), coherence (Chapter 9) and style. Parallelism has the potential to create rhythm, emphasis and drama as it clearly presents ideas or action. Consider this long, graceful (and witty) sentence that begins a magazine article on sneakers:

> A long time ago—before sneaker companies had the marketing clout to spend millions of dollars sponsoring telecasts of the Super Bowl; before street gangs identified themselves by the color of their Adidas; before North Carolina State's basketball players found they could raise a little extra cash by selling the freebie Nikes off their feet; and before a sneaker's very sole had been gelatinized, Energaired, Hexalited, torsioned and injected with pressurized gas—sneakers were, well, sneakers.

First note the obvious parallelism of four clauses beginning with the word *before* and proceeding with similar grammatical patterns. Then note the parallel list of sneaker attributes: *gelatinized, Energaired,* etc. This is writing with pizzazz. It moves; it lilts. It almost makes you interested in sneakers! Of course you noticed the nice bit of word play—the sneaker's very *sole.*

Consider the compact parallelism in the following example from a magazine story about inventive chefs:

> They are serious artists who like to have fun. They may treat desserts as architecture, appetizers as sport, salads as finger painting and main courses as grand opera.

VARY SENTENCE LENGTH

Short sentences are naturally punchy, emphatic and dramatic; long sentences are naturally lilting, rolling and restful. Sentence length communicates just as surely as do the words within the sentence. Writer Sallie Tisdale wanted a blunt, shocking first sentence for her controversial story on women's reproductive freedom. She chose two short, emphatic sentences linked by a semicolon to do the job:

> We do abortions here; that is all we do.

The power of both words and sentence length makes this compelling. On the other hand, consider this 52-word sentence about the creative work of an advertising copywriter who is the subject of an *Esquire* profile:

> He did some memorable commercials in the "McDonald's and You" series, including one marathon spot to launch the campaign, which ran on for as long as a travelogue and had grandparents and riverboats and airplanes and little kids in it, and made you proud, as well as hungry, to be an American.

Note how the sentence construction mirrors the idea the writer is communicating: the marathon length of the McDonald's commercial with its overabundance of kitsch images. The sentence is lilting and playful, seemingly endless (much like a commercial). It has rhythm. You can almost dance to it.

But if you construct a series of sentences of similar lengths, you run the risk of creating a plodding, deadening rhythm. If the sentences are all short, your prose may sound truncated and choppy, like a page from a children's book: "See the ball. The ball is green. Throw the ball." If the sentences are all long, your audience's attention may wander. Varying sentence length helps maintain interest while giving you the opportunity to use rhythm for drama and emphasis. For example, after the 74-word opening sentence of the sneaker article come these short, clipped constructions:

> They were flimsy things, canvas on the top and rubber on the bottom. The lowtops came in white or blue. The hightops came in white or black.

These punchy sentences provide a nice rhythmic balance to the long, rolling introduction. Here's another example of using sentence length to communicate. Note the relatively long sentences followed unexpectedly by a short, clipped sentence at the end.

> Duane Coop is standing twenty feet away from his practice target—a three-foot-diameter log with a painted red bulls-eye— throwing a two-and-a-half pound, thirty-two inch double-bladed ax. The ax makes long, slow, end-over-end revolutions as it sails toward the target. Sprawled under the target, the family cat suns himself, listening without interest to the crack the six-inch blade makes as it slices into the log. The cat figures Duane won't miss. The cat's right.

CONSIDER FRAGMENTS AND RUN-ONS

A fragment (an unfinished piece of a sentence) and a run-on (two or more complete sentences spliced together incorrectly) are grammatical errors. But certain grammatical rules can be bent by knowledgeable writers who are striving to achieve special effects. The rules against fragments and run-ons can occasionally be broken when you have a specific purpose in mind, when your audience (and editor) will stand for it and when the material warrants it. Advertising copywriters seem particularly fragment-prone. They can overdo it, creating choppy, confusing messages. On the other hand, they can use fragments effectively to create surprise and emphasis, as in this Nike ad that plays on a cliché:

> What does a 6'5", 270 lb. defensive lineman do for a workout? Anything he wants.

Anything he wants is a fragment. It's punchy, powerful, funny and appropriate to the subject and medium. It works.

Fragments can create excitement, set a quick pace and grab attention. Like short sentences—but even more so—they have a brisk, staccato beat. They can be tense, dramatic and emphatic. Here is the beginning of a dramatic passage about a writer's experience in Alaska:

> It was 2 p.m. Thirty below. No wind. Totally dark. My boots squeaked on the dry, granular snow as I walked.

These fragments isolate and emphasize parts of the environment and the writer's experience. They (excuse the word play) "freeze frame" certain details, the way a film editor would.

Unlike the staccato beat of fragments, run-ons can communicate a breathless, sing-song rhythm. Depending on the words and ideas, a run-on can quicken the pace with a giddy rush of words or slacken the pace with a languid, rolling motion. Consider this run-on sentence from a *GQ* story about Lawrence Taylor, a former football player with a difficult past:

> When you're welcomed to the University of North Carolina because you played football so well at a small high school in rural Virginia that one school morning you decided to go get drunk and your teacher said go ahead, and then when you get to Chapel Hill, you regularly drink yourself blind, assault people, steal stuff, manipulate your grades and still play on Saturday, still break the Michigan quarterback's leg, and then after you're the second pick overall in the NFL and you start taking drugs in your second year and miss practices and pass out in your car on the Garden State Parkway at 3:30 a.m. and flunk the Breathalyzer and the NFL winks and we shake our heads but scream our lungs out on Sunday when you spear a quarterback in the sternum on a sack, what exactly is supposed to motivate you to change?

That sentence lopes forward, detail after detail, until the litany of Lawrence Taylor's wrongdoings is overpowering. They leave us breathless, just as the sentence itself does. Structure reinforces and enhances message. This is style.

Do remember that breaking grammatical rules is serious business, and that there's an important distinction between breaking a rule purposefully and making a mistake because you don't know the rule. Before you use fragments or run-ons, ask yourself these questions:

- Is the device appropriate to both the subject I am writing about and the medium I am writing for?

- Is this device the best way to achieve the effect I am striving for?

- Does it work?

Don't use fragments or run-ons unless you can answer yes to all three questions. Even then, use these special techniques sparingly. Like all stylistic devices, they lose both meaning and impact if overused.

LISTEN TO THE SOUND OF WORDS

"A sentence is not interesting merely in conveying a meaning of words; it must do something more," wrote poet Robert Frost. "It must convey a meaning by sound." Broadcast journalists and speech writers learn to write for the ear, but print writers often pay little attention to the sounds of the words they choose. That's unfortunate, because most readers *hear* the printed word in their minds as they read. Print writers should be writing for the "inner ear" of their readers. Words chosen and arranged for their sound, as well as their meaning, add style and verve to prose.

Our language is full of words that sound like what they mean. Onomatopoeic words like *crack, buzz, snap, bang* and *chirp* imitate the sound they define. They are crisp, colorful and doubly descriptive. Note how the "liveliness quotient" increases when you choose words for their sound:

instead of <u>complain:</u>	grumble, squawk, growl
instead of <u>fracture:</u>	smash, shatter, snap
instead of <u>talk</u> (a lot):	jabber, yammer, chatter

Some words are not actually onomatopoeic, but their sound adds to their meaning. Words beginning with the *s* sound, for example, often communicate (by sound and meaning) a kind of unpleasantness: *sneer, smirk* and *snigger* are stronger, nastier words than *mock, deride* or *look askance. Entanglements* can be *complications, problems* or *puzzles,* or they can be *snarls* or *snags.* A dog can *dribble* or *drool,* or it can (even more unpleasantly) *slobber* or *slaver.* The meanings are the same; sound adds the extra dimension.

Words beginning with the *k* sound often communicate harshness or force. Politicians can have *power,* but when they have *clout,* you know they're powerful. *Claws* seem more menacing than *talons. Carcass* or *corpse* is a harsher way of saying *dead body.* An ungraceful person is more *awkward* if described as a *clod.* In Chapter 9 we stressed the importance of choosing precise, accurate words. Here we are saying the writer striving for style ought to go one step further. Sound communicates. Look at both the meanings of words and their sounds.

IMAGERY

As writers we are the eyes and ears of our audience. If we do our job well, we should be able to accurately recreate an event, a scene, a person, a moment in time for our audience. If we try harder, if we write with style, we can recreate in such vivid detail that our audience feels it has experienced what we write about. We involve the audience directly. Descriptive detail, showing rather than telling, quotations and anecdotes are all stylistic techniques that can bring the subject close to our audience.

USE DESCRIPTIVE DETAIL

Remember the buildings at Tupperware headquarters that looked like plastic containers? Remember the faces of the couple—colorless and almost round from crying—whose sick dog lay on a steel table? This is descriptive detail. It can be a phrase, a sentence or the makings of an entire scene. Whatever it is, it focuses on particulars, illuminating details that help paint a picture. Consider this description of a house in a longer, biographical piece about its owner.

> Pancho's new house was on the outskirts of town on a half-acre of scorched dirt stubbled with desert weed and brush, an old wooden barn in back, a big, misshapen tamarisk tree in front. It was a squat, ugly, flat-roofed building made of chunks of rock set in concrete troweled over chicken wire. The rock was the color of dried blood.

The details, carefully observed and cleanly written, bring the reader closer.

Descriptive detail can capture an action, paint a scene or help recreate an event. Writer Joan Didion makes readers feel they are looking out the car window when she painstakingly describes this California scene. Note the purposeful use of fragments and manipulation of sentence length to control the rhythm of the passage:

> The way to Banyon is to drive west from San Bernardino out Foothill Boulevard, Route 66: past the Santa Fe switching yards, the Forty Wink Motel. Past the motel that is nineteen stucco teepees: "SLEEP IN A WIGWAM—GET MORE FOR YOUR WAMPUM." Past Fontana Drag City and the Fontana Church of the Nazarene and the Pit Stop A Go-Go; past Kaiser Steel, through Cucamonga, out to the Kapu Kai Restaurant Bar and

Coffee Shop, at the corner of Route 66 and Carnelian Avenue. Up Carnelian Avenue from the Kapu Kai, which means "Forbidden Seas," the subdivision flags whip in the harsh wind.

This descriptive detail is plain and simple. There is a lot of it, but note how little Didion depends on adjectives. This makes the passage crisper and faster paced than it would be otherwise.

SHOW, DON'T TELL

When you *tell* the audience something, you stand between the audience and the subject to offer judgments:

The woman was energetic.

This "descriptive" sentence not only fails to describe, it also obstructs audience involvement. You've observed or talked with the woman and concluded she was energetic. You then *tell* your audience a summary of what you know rather than *show* the woman being energetic and allow the audience to draw its own conclusions. *Showing* involves the audience and helps bridge that gap between audience and experience.

She ran six miles, finished the report and faxed it to the home office, watered the garden, put in a load of laundry, worked on the speech she would be delivering next week and phoned three clients. Then she sat down to breakfast.

Now *that's* energetic.

Gay Talese could have started his story on gangster Frank Costello by telling readers that Costello grew up poor in a New York slum and was now a rich man. Instead, he showed it—crisply, succinctly and with careful detail:

He never dreamed that, as Frank Costello, he would some day spend $50 for a hat, $350 for a suit, and be capable of forgetting $27,200 in the backseat of a New York taxicab.

USE QUOTATIONS

Lively, involving writing almost always includes people. The *Wall Street Journal* discovered this years ago and pioneered a style for writing about complex economic issues. It was deceptively simple: The stories all began with people the reader got to know through description and quotation. A complicated analytical piece on the future of student loans would begin with one student and his story. Those who may have had little initial interest in reading a story about student loans would suddenly find themselves involved in the compelling personal story of a single student. Now hooked, they read on.

One way to bring people to the forefront of a story is to let them talk, to quote them. A quotation is a verbatim statement—the words between the quotation marks are the actual words spoken by the person being quoted. During the information-gathering process, media writers may listen to speeches, attend meetings and conferences, interview by telephone or in person or stand in the background and listen to conversation. All the while, they are scribbling notes or taping or both. When it comes to writing, they can be faced with pages and pages of quotations. How do they decide which quotations to use and which to discard?

The first and most important consideration is *content*. Quoted material, like everything else the writer decides to include, should add to the audience's understanding of the message. The next consideration is *style*. Well-chosen quotations can be powerful elements in a story. They can:

- bring the audience in direct contact with the person
- capture and communicate a person's uniqueness
- contribute to showing rather than telling
- bring personality and passion to issues (even "dull" ones)
- make a person—and a story—come alive

A well-chosen quotation clearly and vividly communicates something about the person. It is brief enough to hold the audience's interest. It expresses an idea that you, the writer, could not have said better. The last criterion is important. Sometimes people are long-winded; sometimes they go off on tangents. If you quote them (unless you are trying to show their long-windedness), you risk boring or confusing your audience. If the material is important enough to include, paraphrase it in your own words. Save quotations for strong, lively material.

But it's not just a quotation that can capture a person's uniqueness and enliven a story, it is how what was said was said, the context. The audience must be placed next to the person, must see and hear the person as he or she speaks. Consider the quotations at the end of this small scene:

> Play has been sluggish in the first quarter. The women seem jittery, distracted, tentative. The coach watches as the opponents score another basket. She balls her hands into tight fists, then calls for a time out. The women gather around her, kneeling in a semi-circle. She folds herself down to their height, then shoves her face a few inches from one of her players. The jugular is bulging down the length of her long neck. "You can play better than this," she shouts at her. "You know how to play better than this."

When the quotation comes, we're ready for it. The scene is set in our minds. Here's another example. Note how journalist Sally Quinn incorporates the contextual material as she goes along. Description and quotation work hand in hand as Quinn introduces the subject of her profile, then 90-year-old Alice Roosevelt Longworth:

> "I still," she muses, rapping her bony fingers against her graying head, "more or less have my, what they call, marbles," and she pulls her flowered shawl around her a little closer, throws her head back and laughs gleefully.

This quotation does everything a good quotation should. The reader can hear the subject talking.

USE ANECDOTES

An anecdote is a short account of an incident, a "mini story" with a beginning, middle and end. An anecdote illustrates a key point in the story or highlights an important theme, offering detail and insight not possible any other way. It *shows* something the writer could have *told*, but in the telling would have weakened. Anecdotes can require a major expenditure of words, and media writers are often strapped for space or time. That's why it is vital to choose wisely, selecting that one moment that reveals, unmasks or captures some quintessential truth about the subject. Here is a well-told anecdote that introduces a New Yorker profile about a sleight-of-hand artist:

> Ricky Jay, who is perhaps the most gifted sleight-of-hand artist alive, was performing magic with a deck of cards. . . . After twenty minutes of disbelief-suspending manipulations, Jay spread the deck face up on the bar counter and asked Nogulich to concentrate on a

specific card but not to reveal it. Jay then assembled the deck face down, shuffled, cut it into two piles, and asked Nogulich to point to one of the piles and name his card.

"Three of clubs," Nogulich said, and he was then instructed to turn over the top card.

He turned over the three of clubs.

Mosher, in what could be interpreted as a passive-aggressive act, quietly announced, "Ricky, you know, I also concentrated on a card."

After an interval of silence, Jay said, "That's interesting, Gregory, but I only do this for one person at a time."

Mosher persisted: "Well, Ricky, I really was thinking of a card."

Jay paused, frowned, stared at Mosher, and said, "This is a distinct change of procedure." A longer pause. "All right—what was the card?"

"Two of spades."

Jay nodded, and gestured toward the other pile, and Mosher turned over its top card.

The deuce of spades.

A small riot ensued.

This anecdote takes a while to relate, but it is worth every word. Imagine the writer just "telling" what the anecdote showed: Ricky Jay does amazing card tricks that astound everyone. Or imagine not seeing Jay in action, but rather reading a summary of his attributes: Ricky Jay is cool and unflappable. It just doesn't work. Well-told anecdotes are the product of superior observation and interviewing skills as well as sophisticated writing skills. They are tough to do, but very much worth the effort. Like descriptive detail, quotations and other "show, don't tell" techniques, anecdotes add zest to your writing.

WRITING WITH STYLE

Style is more than the manipulation of a handful of techniques. It is finding your own "voice"—and it is a lifelong process. Stylish writing and media writing are compatible. Your story or your message will be more forceful and more involving if it is written with verve. Media writing can—and should—make use of an array of techniques designed to make the subject come alive for the audience. Isn't that why we write?

CHAPTER 11

Sense and Sensitivity

Some of the sharpest pain we feel in our lives comes from the words others use against us. Contrary to the old saying about "sticks and stones," names can and do hurt us, sometimes deeply and with lasting consequences. Of course, words themselves do not cause nor can they solve the problems associated with unfair, discriminatory or hurtful treatment of others. But if we consciously or unconsciously use language that insults or that reinforces stereotypes, we help support a world of inequity.

The PC debate—that's "politically correct," not personal computer—has been raging for more than a decade. Frankly, we don't get it. Shouldn't we treat our fellow human beings with respect, both in actions and words? Shouldn't we as writers be sensitive to individual differences? Shouldn't we as mass communicators challenge and break down stereotypes in the interest of learning to live together in an increasingly diverse society?

Of course we should.

Those who rail against using sensitive, appropriate language trivialize the vital concerns of a society (and a world) trying to find ways to adapt to change. They make jokes. Some of them are even funny: "Gee," they smirk, "should we start calling short people *height disadvantaged?* How about people who can't carry a tune? Let's call them *tonally challenged.*" It's certainly true that any reasonable concept can be taken to a ridiculous extreme, as these examples show. The point is that sensitive use of the language is a reasonable concept.

As writers—but more, as citizens—it is our responsibility to use language with compassion. Language should help us appreciate differences among people as it promotes equality and reflects a credo of tolerance. Choosing and using nondiscriminatory language is simple once you attune your sensitivities. Let's consider how to avoid several hurtful "-isms" in writing: sexism, heterosexism, racism, ageism and able-bodiedism.

SEXISM

Sexist language insults, stereotypes or excludes women. It treats men as the norm and women—although they make up 52 percent of the population—as the exception, the "other." Sexist language treats women as inferior to men, thus contributing to both the perception and the reality of inequality between the sexes. Inclusive, nonsexist, nondiscriminatory language, on the other hand, can help create a cultural and political environment that will not support existing inequities. Such language can also reflect the many positive changes that have already happened in the workplace and in the home.

MAN DOES NOT INCLUDE *WOMAN*

One of the most insidious forms of sexism is choosing words meant to refer to both sexes that actually exclude women. We understand the word *man*, for example, to mean a male human being. When we use the same word to mean both male and female human beings (as in "Peace on earth, good will to *men*" or "All *men* are created equal"), we have a problem. How can one word simultaneously support two very different meanings? How can one word be both gender-exclusive (male only) and gender-inclusive (male and female)? It's like saying: Sometimes when I write the word *apple*, I mean apple. But sometimes when I write the word *apple* I mean apple and orange. I leave it to you to figure out which is the operative meaning. It's confusing.

When elementary school girls and boys were asked to draw pictures to accompany a hypothetical history textbook with supposedly gender-inclusive chapter titles like "Colonial Man" and "Democratic Man"—*man* here was supposed to be synonymous with people—they weren't confused at all: All of the boys and just about all of the girls drew pictures of men—male human beings, that is. We may talk about the generic, or gender-inclusive *man*, but in fact, *man* is generally understood as male only.

Our language has a wide variety of inclusive words. When we mean "men and women," we have the language capability to say so. General references should always be inclusive.

Instead of	Use
man, men	person, people
mankind	people
founding fathers	founders, forebears
gentlemen's agreement	informal agreement
manpower	work force
to man (verb)	to staff, operate

THE MYTH OF THE GENERIC *HE*

Just as *man* cannot mean both men only and men and women both, so too *he* cannot refer to a male person at certain times and both genders at other times. When you use *he*, you communicate maleness, whether that is your intention or whether that is the reality. For example:

A journalist must protect <u>his</u> sources.

A child will gain confidence if <u>he</u> is allowed to make <u>his</u> own decisions.

Are all journalists men? Are all children male? Use of *he* or *him* presumes and communicates gender exclusivity. The rule is simple: Never use *he* or *him* unless you are referring to a male. If you mean to be gender-inclusive, you have three choices:

1. When you must use a pronoun to refer to a noun of undetermined or inclusive gender (*journalist, child*), recast the sentence with plurals. *They* and *them* are gender-inclusive.

<u>Journalists</u> must protect <u>their</u> sources.

<u>Children</u> will gain confidence if <u>they</u> are allowed to make <u>their</u> own decisions.

2. If sentence structure or meaning would be impaired by the plural, use *he or she, his or her, him or her*. This construction is a bit awkward—but not as awkward as excluding more than half of the human race.

A journalist must protect <u>his or her</u> sources.

3. Consider whether the pronoun is actually needed. Perhaps the sentence can be rewritten.

A child will gain confidence if allowed to make decisions.

FROM EXCLUSIVE TO INCLUSIVE JOB TITLES

A few hundred feet from a group of workers cutting down roadside brush, you see a sign "Crew at Work." A decade ago, you would have seen "Men at Work." Our language responds to societal change. Jobs that used to be for men only and that carried male-only designations are now filled by both men and women. It is important to use the inclusive job designations. Here are some common ones:

Instead of	Use
mailman	mail carrier
policeman/policemen	police officer, police force
fireman	firefighter
newsman	reporter
businessman	business executive, entrepreneur
salesman	sales clerk, sales representative
foreman	supervisor
congressman	senator, representative
chairman	head, presiding officer, chair
spokesman	representative, leader, spokesperson

CONSISTENT TREATMENT OF THE SEXES

The consistency rule is simply stated and easily followed: When you write about men and women, treat them the same. If you refer to a man by last name only, do so for a woman. If you include such details as marital status, age and physical appearance when writing about a woman, make sure you would do the same if the subject were a man.

Let's say Mr. X is your state's new governor. Would you consider writing:

With his flashing brown eyes and warm, gracious smile, a svelte Mr. X, grandfather of four, moved into the governor's mansion yesterday.

It sounds ridiculous, doesn't it? But, because of deep-seated sexism that allows women to be judged by different criteria than men, a female governor might very well be referred to this way. How about a sports story in which the new women's basketball coach is described as a "curly-headed blonde"? Just imagine using similar physical description for the male coach. It is laughable. If it would be inappropriate to offer this information about a man, it is equally inappropriate to offer it about a woman.

Contrary to the cliché, consistency is not the hobgoblin of small minds. It is a tool for nonsexist writing. Concern yourself particularly with consistency in these five areas:

1. *Titles, names and references.* *Ms.*, which signals that the person named is female, but unlike *Miss* or *Mrs.* does not give information about her marital status, is the courtesy title of choice for women. It parallels *Mr.*, which signals maleness without marital status. When you use one, use the other. If you use titles like *Pres., Sen.* or *Rev.* to refer to a man, refer to a woman the same way.

   Increasingly, publications are doing away with most courtesy titles, especially on second reference. In that case, refer to both men and women by last names only, except when you are writing about a couple who share the same last name. Then full names, first names or courtesy titles (used equally for both halves of the couple) will provide clarity. Some writers like the informality of referring to people by their first names. If the story warrants such a tone and the publication allows for this style, first names should be used consistently for the sexes. Do not write "Mr. Donnell and his assistant Cheryl."

2. *Marital status and children.* Sometimes a person's marital or parental status is an appropriate and important piece of information that should be included in the story. Too often, though, women are defined by marital and parental status and men are not. Test yourself: If you would include the information for a man, then do so for a woman.

   Rain City real estate developer Robert Dant has just finalized a multimillion-dollar deal to refurbish the historic Smith building. Dant, father of three and husband of computer executive Patricia Miller, . . .

   Sound ridiculous?

3. *Physical appearance.* Physical appearance may be completely appropriate to a story. Everyone wants to know how tall the new basketball center is (male or female). The overweight diet doctor, the mayor who wears Birkenstocks—these are all appropriate descriptions that add to readers' understanding. But too often, women's clothes, bodies and mannerisms are described regardless of their relevance to the story. Women are not objects to be inspected and evaluated; they are, like men, subjects to be written about.

4. *Adding gender.* Most nouns in the English language are gender-inclusive: *writer, author, artist, scientist, doctor.* Treat them as such. Just as you do not need to insert *male* or *man* in front of these nouns when referring to a man in these positions, you should not insert *female* or *woman* when referring to a woman. You would probably never consider writing "*male* author Stephen King." Why then do we often see such constructions as "*female* novelist Anne Rice"? Too frequently, writers add female gender to nouns that are actually gender-inclusive. The implied message: Only men are authors, artists, writers, etc. A woman is the rare exception.

5. *Equal treatment in word pairs.* When you pair men and women, make sure you choose equal words to refer to both sexes. Adult males and females are *men* and *women;* children are *boys* and *girls.*

Instead of	Use
man and wife	husband and wife
man and lady	man and woman; gentleman and lady
men and girls	boys and girls

DEMEANING OR STEREOTYPICAL WORDS

Beware of words that imply stereotypes. For example, a spirited, competitive, athletic girl is often called a *tomboy,* as if no girl could have these qualities. Having good manners is considered *ladylike.* But is being polite a sex-linked characteristic? A male student is called a *student;* a female student is often called a *coed.* This abbreviation of the word *coeducational* once again takes the male as standard and the female as deviation. That is, an institution becomes coeducational when women join. The "normal" college student is a man. Using this logic in reverse, the men now attending traditional female-only colleges should be called coeds. Could you imagine writing "Dirk Asbury, a Vassar coed"? Forget *coed;* students are students.

HETEROSEXISM

Discriminatory or stereotypical language exists for any group whose physical appearance, behavior or beliefs vary from those in the mainstream. Homosexuals have traditionally had a very difficult time swimming against that tide, and our language proves the point. We have dozens of words that insult and demean gay men and lesbians (*fag, fairy, dyke, butch*) and many more meant to tease and torment any woman who exhibits traditionally male behavior and any man who does not. Consider the simple ways writers can rid their language of bias and bigotry.

NOT EVERYONE IS HETEROSEXUAL

Just as sexist language assumes maleness, heterosexist language assumes wholesale heterosexuality. But everyone is not heterosexual. Several decades of research, both scientific and historical, have shown that about 10 percent of the population—now as well as centuries ago—is homosexual. That means one in 10 of your readers (your colleagues, the writers you admire, the merchants you deal with) is gay. Because homosexuality has carried such a stigma in our society, few gay men and lesbians (until very recently) have gone public with their sexual orientations. Thus many of us have grown up thinking of homosexuality as a rare occurrence. It isn't.

If you don't immediately assume the heterosexuality of those you write about, you can avoid awkwardness (for example, asking an interview subject why he or she never married) and surprise (upon learning, for example, that a "feminine-looking" woman is a lesbian).

A PERSON IS NOT HIS OR HER SEXUAL ORIENTATION

Although a person's sexual orientation may be vital to the story—a profile of a gay activist, a church and its homosexual parishioners—many times it is not. If you would not consider writing "The company owned by heterosexual entrepreneur Leslie Morse . . ." then why routinely include information about homosexual orientation? Even worse is such wording as "an admitted homosexual" (as if the person were admitting to a heinous offense) or a "practicing homosexual." (Do we ask heterosexuals whether they "practice" too?)

BEWARE OF STEREOTYPES AND EXCEPTIONS

Homosexuals cannot be stereotyped any more than can heterosexuals. They are all ages, all races and ethnicities, all religions. They live in different parts of the country and are employed in all occupations. Some are single; others live with lifelong partners. Some have children; others do not.

It is important to understand and appreciate this diversity for two reasons. First, it will help you avoid thinking of (and describing) a gay person as "a type." Second, and probably more important, it will help you guard against making a point of characteristics that don't conform to the type, calling special attention to such "oddities" as the lesbian with long hair or the gay man with children. The assumption behind these observations is that all lesbians look a certain way, that all gay men live a certain kind of life. Do all heterosexuals look and act the same?

RACISM

Those Americans of African, Asian, Native American or Hispanic descent—that is, those who look noticeably different than Americans of European descent—are the most obvious victims of racist attitudes, behavior and speech. Racism can affect every part of their lives, from where they live to the medical services they receive, from the quality of their education to their self-esteem and self-image. Racism is a problem of enormous proportion in the U.S. (and worldwide). Americans of various European ancestry labor under the burden of ethnic stereotypes: the mobster Italian, the arrogant German, the dumb Pole, the miserly Jew. There are more than enough negative and hurtful slurs to go around.

It is unlikely that you would ever practice overt racism in print. But it is likely that your judgment would be affected by the long-standing and pervasive stereotypes that exist in our society. Regardless of your own personal good will, you assuredly harbor some prejudices; you undoubtedly "see" people through the filter of stereotype. Here is how to make sure your language is prejudice-free.

IDENTIFYING PEOPLE BY RACE

Do not identify a person's race or ethnicity unless it is a vital part of the story. If someone is the first of his or her racial or ethnic group to achieve a certain goal, that fact may be newsworthy (although those "first . . . who" stories can quickly become trite). But if you would not normally identify a person as being *white* in a story, do not use racial identity at all. For example, if you would not write:

Dan Rather, the white anchor of the "CBS Nightly News". . .

Then do not write:

Connie Chung, noted Asian-American newscaster . . .

Relatively few situations require the inclusion of race.

REINFORCING STEREOTYPES BY "EXCEPTIONS"

Language can reinforce racism by treating people as exceptions to stereotypes, which is just as demeaning and insulting as using the stereotype itself. For example, making it a point to call an Italian-American "respectable and law-abiding" implies that most are not, thus reinforcing the Mafia stereotype. Writing that a Mexican-American is "hard-working and even-tempered" implies that Mexican-Americans in general are indolent and volatile—but this one is an exception. The negative stereotype is embedded in the "positive" attributes.

BEWARE OF EURO-CENTRISM

When you write that someone is "culturally deprived" or "culturally disadvantaged," what are you saying? The message is clear (especially to the "deprived"): White, European culture is superior; those who grow up outside of it are at a loss. Is an American Indian child who grows up learning the culture, language and traditions of his or her tribe "culturally deprived"? Why is a racial or ethnic minority considered culturally deprived because of lack of involvement or exposure to white culture but a white person is not considered culturally deprived because of lack of involvement or exposure to other racial or ethnic cultures?

Eurocentrism—using white, European culture as the standard—is also evident when you refer to people as "non-whites." Why describe people by what they aren't? Would you call a 25-year-old a "non-teen"? Would you call a brunette a "non-blond"? Of course not. Be particularly careful when using the word *minority* as well. In a growing number of U.S. cities, in the state of California and in the world in general, whites are the minority.

SENSITIVITY TO GROUP NAMES

Be aware of what members of various racial and ethnic groups call themselves and want to be publicly referred to as. These names change with the times. Early in the 20th century, black Americans were called *coloreds* and pressed hard to be called the more respectable term, *Negro*. In the 1960s, *black* and *Afro-American* were the terms of choice. Today, many people prefer *African-American*, a term consistent with how we refer to other Americans of international heritage (*Asian-Americans,* for example). Indians are generally referred to as *American Indians* or *Native Americans* or as members of particular tribes or confederations. Those descended from Spanish-speaking cultures might be referred to as *Chicano(a), Latino(a), Hispanic* or, more specifically, by country of origin (*Cuban-American, Mexican-American*).

Given that the word *minorities* may be factually inaccurate and that *non-whites* is Eurocentric, the search continues for a more sensitive aggregate term. *People of color* is a current favorite, although some people find it less than acceptable. It may also be somewhat less than accurate, as olive-skinned whites of Mediterranean ancestry can be more "colorful" than some people of color. Rather than lumping together a variety of racial and ethnic groups and hunting for a single descriptor, it seems preferable to list the groups themselves.

AGEISM

Codger, fogy, fossil. Geezer, duffer, coot. Hag, nag, bag, crone. The Geritol for lunch bunch. Senile citizens. Our language is not kind to older people.

Older people are feeble, frail and forgetful, crabby, creaky, constipated and curmudgeonly. These are the stereotypes, and they are insulting and inaccurate. The vast majority of older people live healthy, productive and independent lives. The active, alert, involved older person is the rule, not the exception.

As people live longer and as that huge demographic blip known as the baby boom moves through middle and then old age, the numbers of older Americans will increase dramatically. At the turn of the century, one in 16 Americans was 60 or older. Today it's one in six. Within 20 years, it will be one in four. It is past time for writers to learn how to deal accurately and sensitively with older people.

Few writers would actually use any of the offensive terms listed at the beginning of this section, but many might find the stereotypes pervading their writing in more subtle ways. Generally, ageist language reinforces damaging stereotypes by expressing great surprise over those who do not conform to them.

She is still vigorous at 70.

His mind is still sharp at 75.

The implication is that most 70-year-olds lack vigor and that most 75-year-olds are senile. If you refuse to accept the inaccurate stereotypes, you will avoid making insulting statements about "exceptions."

Although our society (and its language and images) is unkind to older people of both genders, more women than men may be victimized by ageist language. The stigma of aging is greater for women, who, throughout their lives, have traditionally been evaluated more by what they look like than by who they are. A gray-haired or balding man of 65 might be thought of and described as "distinguished" or "at the height of his powers." A gray-haired woman of 65 is rarely thought of or described in such complimentary terms.

Ageism exists on both ends of the life span. Teenagers are irresponsible, inarticulate, hormone-driven slackers—or so goes the stereotype. That accounts for the ageist singling out of "responsible" and "thoughtful" teens, as if they were the surprising exception rather than, in fact, the rule.

To write sensitively and accurately about those in any age group, question your assumptions and reject stereotypes. Write about people as individuals, not as representatives of, or exceptions to, their age group.

"ABLE-BODIEDISM"

No, that is not a word, and we are not suggesting that it should be. "Able-bodiedism" is a term we've coined here to stand for language discrimination against people who have disabilities. Tens of thousands of Americans have physical or mental disabilities, some of which limit their activities and impair their performance, some of which do not.

A disability does not necessarily "disable" or make one a "disabled person." Some disabilities simply don't affect one's work. (Is the writer in a wheelchair a "disabled writer"?) Other disabilities, in fact, create new abilities.

Consider, for example, the blind or sight-impaired person who has developed supernormal hearing abilities. If you consider the loss of sight, the person is "disabled." If you consider the gain in hearing, the person is more able-bodied than most. What about the deaf or hearing-impaired person who reads lips and communicates through sign language? If that person is "disabled," aren't hearing people "sign-language-impaired"?

When writing about people with physical or mental limitations, ask them how they want to be referred to. Also, keep in mind this vital rule: People are not their handicaps. People *have* handicaps (limits, impairments, different abilities). Never write:

Arthur Thomas, an epileptic . . .

The handicapped children . . .

Write instead:

Arthur Thomas, who has epilepsy . . .

The children, who all have handicaps . . .

THE -ISMS GOLDEN RULE

All advice boils down to one rule: Write about others as you would want them to write about you. You see yourself as an individual who may be male or female, old or young, fat or thin, black, brown or white. But these and other characteristics don't overshadow who you are personally and professionally. See—and write about—others with the same regard for and sensitivity to their individuality. This is not a matter of being "politically correct." It is a matter of being human.

Topical Guide to Grammar and Word Use

Readers of the many editions of "When Words Collide" have frequently told us how much they appreciate Part 2 for its accessibility and its sensible guidance. We're pleased that this book has become such a useful reference tool; however, we say this in the hope that you'll remember the importance of Part 1 with its longer, more involved explanations!

The guiding principle in this section is that good writers need rules. Indeed, skilled writers realize that they have a strong ally in correct, well-focused usage that helps them reach their audiences with clarity and precision. These writers don't see the rules of grammar as being elitist and exclusionary; they see them as being critical to providing information with unmistakable meaning.

In an attempt to provide a quick reference on grammar and word use issues, we offer Part 2. The entries in this section are starting points for decisions on grammatical correctness, and they direct you to longer discussions, if needed.

We offer these entries with the following premises:

- Writing is more precise—and therefore somewhat more formal—than our everyday speech.

- Changes in standards for written communication occur more slowly—and thoughtfully—than for the spoken word.

- Rules of grammar and usage are based on logic, meaning and long-standing practice.

It is true that some style guides are too authoritarian, perhaps even eccentric at times. On the other hand, some contemporary dictionaries are taking anarchy to new levels: They seem to accept so many definitions and uses of words that it becomes almost impossible to maintain the proper shades of meaning and nuances of those words. This guide recognizes the volatility of our language, but it urges caution in adopting trendy spoken standards. It is an alphabetical reference that addresses usage issues as well as grammatical terms and problems. Where appropriate, the reader is given a page citation in Part 1 for deeper examination and discussion. We hope that this guide will challenge you to maintain proper usage and meaning as you seek new and creative ways to improve your expression.

Just as careful, concerned writers struggle to avoid jargon, clutter and euphemisms in their writing, so too should they strive for the highest level of precision in their meanings. To the charge that we want to preserve distinctive meanings of words, we plead guilty. We hope you'll join the crusade.

-able/-ible endings   These suffixes (endings to root words) can be frustrating to the challenged speller. Why do we have *acceptable* on one hand and *impossible* on the other? Well, as Chapter 8 reminds you, a lot of imprinting is necessary to avoid the wrong suffix choice. Remember that *-able* endings are more common and that in most cases, the *-able* suffix is attached to complete root words (*change + able = changeable*). Also see p. 131 for that list of pesky words!

active voice/passive voice   *Voice* refers to the form of a verb as it relates to its subject. When the subject of the sentence performs the action ("The Second Fidelity Bank ceased operation"), the verb (*ceased*) is in the *active voice*. If the subject receives the action of the verb ("The suspects were caught in the hospital's laundry room"), the verb (*were caught*) is in the *passive voice*. Generally the active voice is stronger and more direct than the passive voice. Too much dependence on the passive voice can rob your sentences of needed strength. It may also cover up a poor reporting job. However, there are reasons to use the passive, especially when you need to stress the receiver of action rather than the performer. See Chapter 6 for a complete discussion of voice.

adjective   This part of speech is a "finishing touch" for a noun or pronoun. As a modifier, the adjective describes, limits and adds important detail. In certain structures it can have the "feel" of a verb (that's why it's sometimes called a *participle*). The writer's biggest problem with adjectives is choosing the most precise ones. For example, why write

The stranger's clothes were <u>torn</u> and <u>dirty.</u>

when you could be more descriptive with

The stranger wore a <u>tattered</u> denim shirt, and his trousers were crusted with a <u>foul,</u> <u>swampy</u> residue.

Adjectives are the hue and chroma of our writing. The spectrum of color they can provide is almost limitless!

adverb Remember that not all adverbs end in *-ly!* That would be much too simple. Adverb means literally "near the verb." However, in expressing matters of degree, time, place and manner, the adverb can modify not only verbs but also adjectives and other adverbs. Adverbs generally answer *how, why* and *when.* Like the adjective, the adverb must be chosen carefully and applied precisely. For example, why write

The stock market fell <u>sharply</u> today.

when you could add more power with

The stock market tumbled <u>wildly</u> today.

Strong adverbs work in tandem with descriptive verbs to create powerful imagery.

adverse/averse Although these adjectives sound alike, they have distinct meanings. *Adverse,* which means "unfavorable or hostile," is used best when it modifies an adjacent noun that refers to a thing or concept:

The senators did not expect such <u>adverse</u> reaction to the defense bill.

However, if you want to describe someone's reluctance to do something, you should use *averse:*

Dennis Rodman never was <u>averse</u> to acting outrageously.

affect/effect A pox on this pair! The improper selection of one for the other is one of the most common writing faults today. There seem to be two reasons for the confusion about these words: (1) They sound alike, and (2) some writers don't understand what part of speech each is. If you remember that *affect* is almost always a verb that means "to influence or to pretend to have," you can see how different it is from *effect*, which is almost always a noun that means "result." Examples:

The president's program will <u>affect</u> millions of welfare recipients. (verb: "to influence")

The prisoner <u>affected</u> a carefree manner. (verb: "to pretend to have")

The senator questioned the <u>effect</u> of the welfare cutback. (noun: "result")

Effect is occasionally used as a verb in formal writing to mean "to bring about."

Top management <u>effected</u> some personnel changes.

This is awkward usage. You see this use in stuffy business writing; it is inappropriate for journalistic writing. *Affect* can also be a noun in very narrow usage to denote certain behavior in psychology. Forget both of these usages unless you need to use and explain them in a direct quote. We don't want to sound too dogmatic about a language that should be flexible, but we think it's warranted in this case. (So—how are the <u>effects</u> of all this grammar and word-use discussion <u>affecting</u> you so far?)

-aholic endings Here is proof that language indeed lives, *-aholic* words have recently entered our vocabulary. Through slang usage, *-aholic* tacked onto a word has come to mean "one obsessed by," as in *workaholic* and *chocaholic*. Presumably these new words owe their existence to *alcoholic*. But instead of taking the accepted suffix *-ic,* meaning "of or pertaining to," from the root word *alcohol,* whoever created those new words stole (and misspelled) another syllable and a half. That this linguistic configuration makes no sense bothers only purists. The rest of us enjoy new words with distinct meanings.

aid/aide Don't be fooled: *Aides* ("assistants") give *aid* ("help, assistance") to their bosses. *Aid* also can be a verb, but *aide* can only be a noun. So, constructions such as "the president's aide" and "giving aid and comfort to the enemy" are correct.

all/any/most/some These can be singular or plural. If the word carries the meaning of "general amount or quantity," the meaning is singular:

<u>All</u> of the contraband <u>was</u> seized at the port.

<u>Some</u> of his testimony <u>was</u> stricken from the record.

If you can read "individual and number" into the sentence, the plural verb should be used.

All of the passengers <u>were</u> rescued.
Have <u>any</u> of their relatives been notified?

See p. 62 and the entry for *none.*

AL–AN

allude/elude These meanings shouldn't elude you. If you are making an "indirect reference" to something, you *allude* to it. (If you want to mention it directly, you *refer* to it.)

The candidate <u>alluded</u> to the prison record of his opponent.

Elude is your choice if you mean "to escape or to avoid detection."

The fugitive <u>eluded</u> the search party for two weeks.

among/between These two prepositions will probably always confuse us. In our reverie about the simple days of grade school, we sometimes recall this bit of errant dogma: *Among* relates to more than two persons or things, and *between* applies to only two. We soon discovered, of course, that nothing in life could be that simple. The archaic meaning of *between* was "by the twain," or "by two." It implies separation or connection involving two entities. *Among* implies a "distribution" involving greater generally undefined numbers. The rule today is this: If there is a "definite relation" involved, *between* is preferred, no matter what the number.

<u>Between</u> you and me, this business will never succeed.
Negotiations have broken down <u>between</u> the government mediator, autoworkers and management.

Among is properly used where there is no explicit relationship stated and when distribution is stressed.

The handbills were passed out <u>among</u> the crowd.
The reward money was divided <u>among</u> the four families who supplied clues to the police department.

Chances are you'll be using *between* more than *among* in your writing. One other point about these prepositions: Remember that if they are used in a simple prepositional phrase, their objects and personal pronouns will be in the objective case. For more on this, see p. 76.

antecedents Often hiding in sentences like serpents in tall grass, these words are reference "homes" for the pronouns that follow. Because the antecedent of a pronoun sometimes is unclear, writers may have problems with number and person agreement. In the following sentences, proper antecedents are underlined:

> Sarah is one of those <u>people</u> who never require more than four hours' sleep. (Why is the antecedent *people* instead of *one*? Because the sentence tells us that there is more than one person who can get by on that amount of sleep. Therefore, that clause needs a plural verb, as people *require*.)
>
> Zane is the <u>only one</u> of the finalists who isn't nervous.
> (In this sentence, only one finalist isn't nervous, hence the singular verb.)
>
> Gerry's <u>theory</u> is intriguing, but not many of his colleagues agree with it. (The pronoun *it* properly refers to the antecedent *theory*. The intriguing theory not Gerry, is the focus.)

Because having to search for proper antecedents can be annoying or distracting, writers should take special care that the pronoun-antecedent relationship is clear.

a number of/the number of   The intended number of these phrases depends on a simple article. If the article is *a,* the meaning is plural:

> <u>A number</u> of senators <u>have</u> left the assembly.

If the article is *the,* the meaning is more indefinite (or is seen as a unit) and therefore is singular:

> <u>The number</u> of deadly tornadoes in the South <u>has</u> increased recently.

These phrases illustrate an easy-to-remember tip about subject-verb agreement: If the phrase or word denotes "a general amount or quantity," the verb is singular; if the phrase or word denotes "a more definable number of individuals," the verb is plural. See p. 59.

anxious/eager   This choice causes more anxiety than eagerness. It shouldn't if you remember that you can only be anxious *about* something; you cannot be anxious *to do* that thing. *Anxious* implies fear and worry.

> The mayor says she is <u>anxious</u> about the outcome of the election.

If you are stimulated and excited at the prospect of doing something, then you are *eager* to do it.

> Norman is <u>eager to</u> review the registrations at the Bates Motel.

appositive   This is a word, phrase or clause placed in the same grammatical relationship as the word that precedes it. Words in apposition have a "side-by-side" relationship. They are important to identify because they have some bearing on punctuation and case decisions. For example, a *restrictive* appositive is one that is essential to the meaning of a sentence and thus requires no commas:

AS

My friend John helped write headlines while his friend Susan
(appositive)   (appositive)
finished the design. (A comma would not be correct after *friend* because *John* and *Susan* are essential to the meaning of the subject.)

A *nonrestrictive* appositive still has a side-by-side relationship, but its meaning is not essential to the sentence. It must be set off by commas:

Mullins, a proven clutch player, has a secure place on the roster.
(appositive)

as if/like Advertising slogans to the contrary, don't look for the preposition *like* to join the lofty company of the conjunction. *As if* is properly used as a conjunction if it introduces a clause:

It looks as if it will rain.

Like, a preposition, takes a simple object; it cannot introduce a clause.

It looks like rain.

Some grammarians say that *like* may evolve into a conjunction. We hope that will be an extraordinarily long process, spanning several geological ages.

as/than They can be both prepositions and conjunctions. This can cause problems with case selection. If these words are used as conjunctions, most likely they are used to make comparisons. If so, the nominative case of the pronoun is needed.

There's no one more handsome than he.
("Than he is handsome" is understood as the second clause.)
Please do as I have instructed.

However, *as* and *than* can also be prepositions.

Why did you pick Beth rather than her?
Do you really think you can pose as me in the parade?

Obviously, no comparisons are being made here. The pronouns following these prepositions must be in the objective case.

as well as This phrase, which connects a subordinate thought to the main one, can cause agreement problems between subject and verb.

Remember that the main subject—not any word or phrase parenthetical to it—controls the number and the person of the verb.

The <u>house,</u> as well as its contents, <u>was destroyed</u> in the early morning fire.

<u>I,</u> as well as you, <u>am</u> reluctant to sue.

Similar parenthetical phrases are *together with, in addition to* and *along with.* You'll find it easier to isolate the true subject of the sentence if you set off these phrases with commas. See p. 60.

bad/badly   Don't feel bad if you use these words badly! *Bad* is an adjective. In linking verb constructions in which you want to describe the subject, *bad* is the correct choice.

Mayor Gaydos said he <u>felt</u> <u>bad</u> about the bond issue defeat.
       (l.v.) (adj.)

This sentence describes the mayor's state of being, not his physical ability to feel. When you describe some quality of the verb instead of the subject, you use the adverb *badly.*

The prime minister <u>took</u> her defeat <u>badly</u>.
       (verb)   (adv.)
(*Badly* describes the verb *took,* not the noun *prime minister.*)

because of/due to   You should always use *because of* when matching cause to effect. It is used when the writer can ask *why* in a sentence.

The stock market crashed <u>because of</u> panic selling.
<u>Because</u> of an increase in wholesale prices for jack cheese, Taco Rapido increased the cost of its burritos.

Due to should never be used in anything but a linking verb construction. *Due* is an adjective; its preposition *to* relates to the condition of a subject.

The increase in the cost of burritos <u>is due to</u> soaring prices of jack cheese.

Note that you can't ask *why* in this type of construction. But you can in the next sentence, and that is why *due to* is incorrect:

(Due to/<u>Because of</u>) the budget shortfall this year, no new grant applications will be accepted.

beside/besides   *Beside* means "next to" or "at the side of." *Besides* means "in addition to."

The nervous guard stood <u>beside</u> the visiting dignitary.
(next to)
<u>Besides</u> Harry and me, only Sarah knew of the escape plan.
(in addition to)

Remember that simple objects of these prepositions take the objective case.

bi-/semi- *Bi-* means "two," and *semi-* means "half." This distinction works fine until you come to calculating years.

bimonthly—every two months
semimonthly—twice a month

If you mean something that happens twice a year, use *semiannual* rather than *biannual,* even though the dictionary recognizes both. That will avoid confusion with *biennial* (something that happens every two years). Note that the prefixes *bi-* and *semi-* are hyphenated only when the word that follows them begins with an *i* or is capitalized.

both/few/many/several These indefinite pronouns always take a plural verb. See p. 61.

brand names/trademarks These are business-created words that have not fallen into generic usage. Do you really want to refer to a specific product, or do you just want to mention the process? If you want to mention the process or the generic name, avoid brand name reference. Do not write, for example,

The spy xeroxed all the documents.

For one thing, *Xerox,* a registered trade name, isn't a verb; the spy can photocopy the documents, but he or she can't *xerox, canonize* or *savinize* them. Other examples are *Scotch tape* (a brand of cellophane tape), *Coke* (one of many cola beverages), *Mace* (a brand of tear gas) and *Kleenex* (a brand of facial tissue). All brand names and trademarks should be capitalized.

bureaucratese/jargon These words and phrases, used by government workers, sports writers, scientists, doctors, computer programmers and a host of other professionals, give proof that our language is dynamic, although occasionally both imprecise and inefficient. Jargon has changed our language—but not for the better. It often weakens the economy of our writing. For example, you no longer measure the effect of deficit spending on a budget; you ascertain how the program will *impact on fiscal planning.* You no longer evaluate things; you *effect a needs assessment.* You no longer say *now* or *today;* it is *at this point* *in time.* A heart attack becomes an *M.I.* (myocardial infarct). A stroke becomes a *C.V.A.* (cerebral vascular accident). And a sports team doesn't defeat another one; it *rips, tears, repels, devours* (*dices, peels, juliennes?*) the visiting Huskies, Spartans or what have you. Perhaps the culprit is poor word selection. Using words that reflect our trendiness, our desire to be at the vanguard of new expressions, creates a barrier to clear communication. These words sock in the borders of our expression with a fog of our own making.

but It is most frequently a conjunction, connecting words and phrases of equal rank and implying a contrast between those elements. It almost always requires a comma between the clauses it separates.

> The commissioners approved the budget resolution, <u>but</u> they denied a room tax provision for that document.

But also can be a preposition meaning "except."

> Everybody <u>but</u> me went to the party.

Note that the objective case is required for the pronoun when it relates to the preposition.

Can *but* be used to begin a sentence, like the conjunctive adverb *however?* Of course, if you don't overdo it. Just remember it's meant to coordinate clauses. But who are we to be so dogmatic about grammar?

can/may Please preserve the distinctiveness of this pair! *Can* denotes ability, and *may* denotes possibility and permission. If your sentence is in the form of a question, *may* is almost always your choice:

> <u>May</u> I go to the exhibit?

"*Can* he go to the exhibit?" has nothing to do with his ability to do anything, although "Do you think I *can* win this election?" is correct usage because it asks for confidence in one's ability to do something. This, too, would be correct:

> She <u>can</u> run the 200 meters faster than any of her teammates.

Some stylebook authorities have thrown in the towel on the interchangeability of *can* and *may.* Don't give up on these two; they're worth the fight. Postscript: Remember that *may* also can express possibility.

> I *may* buy that new boat we've been talking about.

careen This word often falls victim to imprecise usage. Unless it is leaning sideways or tossing about like a boat under sail, a car that is out of control doesn't *careen* into a crowd of shoppers. It might speed, skid or veer, but it rarely will take a nautical lean, balancing nicely on two wheels en route to an insurance claim.

CA–CL

case Understanding case helps explain why *who* rather than *whom, us* rather than *we,* and *s'* are needed in certain sentences. The three cases are nominative, objective and possessive. Certain pronouns change their form to accommodate a change in case, and nouns change only in their possessive case. See Chapter 5.

censor/censure These words both perform negative, though different, actions. You can *censor* materials by screening, changing or forbidding them.

> The press officer <u>censored</u> all dispatches from the battle lines.

You generally can only *censure* people—by condemning them or expressing disapproval of their actions.

> The senators <u>censured</u> their colleague because he attempted to <u>censor</u> his staff report on the budget.

These words can also be nouns. So, you can have an "official government censor" as well as a "resolution of censure." Spelling note: They sound like *censer* (a container used to burn incense) and *sensor* (a photoelectric cell).

chair/chairperson Despite protestations of old-line grammarians who cry out for tradition and purity, we feel the term *chairman* unfairly and incorrectly assumes maleness of that position. It is one of many such terms in our language. For years, authoritative dictionaries have referred to *chair* as "a person who presides over a meeting" and "an office or position of authority." A person—man or woman—can chair a meeting or be a program chair. It assumes nothing but the position itself. Because the words seem contrived and awkward, avoid *chairer* and *chairperson.* However, some news organizations now are using the official title of the position in their stories, no matter how awkward it may seem. See Chapter 11.

clause This is a group of words that contains both a subject and a verb. Although that may sound like the definition of a sentence, not all clauses are complete thoughts. *Independent clauses* express complete thoughts and can stand alone as sentences, as in

> <u>The California Supreme Court</u> <u>handed</u> Democrats
> (subj.)   (verb)
> a major victory yesterday.

Dependent clauses have subjects and verbs, but their meaning is incomplete because they may contain a relative pronoun that traces its meaning to the independent clause, as in this attachment to the previous sentence:

CL–CO

> ... that should guarantee them a majority in the Assembly.
> (rel. pron. as subj.) (verb)

So, in these examples, we have one sentence with two clauses. Rather than creating two sentences, a writer may choose to keep a principal thought in one construction by making one thought dominant (independent) and the other subordinate (dependent). See p. 44.

clutter   This is the excess baggage that obscures clarity in writing. With clutter, thoughts are unfocused. Phrase is tacked onto phrase, forcing clauses into a line of uneven thought. Packing too much into a sentence—something that happens often in writing a summary news lead—produces clutter:

> A spectator knifed the referee to death after a soccer match at Bosanski Milosevac, near Modrica in Central Yugoslavia, the Belgrade tabloid *Vecernje Novosti* reported Saturday.

Simpler sentences and shorter paragraphs can reduce clutter:

> Is one player strong enough to lift a team to the top of the college basketball world?
> Perhaps—if his name is Sampson.

collective nouns   Their singular forms denote a group of people or things—for example, *jury, herd, athletics* and *politics.* They can be troublesome for subject-verb agreement. If the noun is considered as a whole, the verb and associated pronouns are singular:

> The jury has returned its verdict.

If that unit is broken up or considered individually, the plural verb is required:

> The herd of cattle have scattered because of the dust storm.

Although the preceding sentence is correct, it sounds awkward because of the idea of *herd.* If the cattle were split up, they are not the same herd. It would sound better to write, "The cattle have scattered. . . ." See p. 62.

collision   This is a violent contact between *moving* bodies. An accident between a moving car and a stationary telephone pole is not a collision; it is a *crash*. An oil tanker does not collide with a bridge or a reef. In a more figurative sense, ideas, opinions and, yes, words can collide.

colon This punctuation mark (:) introduces thoughts, quotations or a series. Capitalize matter following a colon only if it can stand alone as a sentence. So:

> Her parting thought to the committee would haunt them for many years: You can't build a budget on deficit spending.
> Besides cartooning, Charles Schulz has one great passion: hockey.

comma splice This is also known as *comma fault*. It occurs at two levels of composition. It may be a mistake by the careless writer who joins two independent clauses without either a coordinating conjunction or a semicolon. Or it may be a device by the accomplished writer who does not want the harsh stop of a semicolon to slow the meter of a sentence. These are unacceptable comma splices:

> The council approved the resolution, the mayor vetoed it the next day.
> (The sentence lacks the conjunction *but* or a semicolon between clauses.)
> He enjoys reviewing movies, however, he says he can't waste his time on "trash like this."
> (Presence of the conjunctive adverb *however* requires a semicolon between clauses—that is, between movies and however.)

In short sentences the comma splice has received the blessing of most grammarians. "You'll like her, she's a Leo" can survive without a conjunction or semicolon. Like the sentence fragment, the comma splice should be used sparingly—and by writers who know when they are using it!

compared to/compared with These are about as interchangeable as American and European electric voltage. When you liken one thing to another, you must use *compared to*:

> The governor <u>compared</u> the logging of pristine, old-growth timber <u>to</u> taking a thoroughbred racehorse and chopping it into lunch meat.

When you place items side by side to examine their similarities and differences, you must use *compared with*:

> Interest rates have fallen to 5.5 percent, <u>compared with</u> the 1980 rate of 14 percent.

As you can see, the use of *compared to* is figurative and metaphorical. Not so *compared with*—it's statistical rather than creative. Whereas you might compare today's weather *to* a joyous song of hope, you can examine facts and compare last winter's rainfall *with* the winter rain in 1899.

complement/compliment They both can be nouns or verbs. *Complement* is defined as "that which completes something, supplements it or brings it to perfection." That is quite different from *compliment*, which means "an expression of praise or admiration." So, a hat may complement a suit, but you would compliment the wearer on his or her hat.

compose/comprise *Compose* is not as direct as *comprise*. Something is *composed of* other things (made up of); however, one thing *comprises* (takes in, includes) other things. The following are correct usages:

> His salad dressing was <u>composed of</u> olive oil, balsamic vinegar and puree of turnip.
> Her speech <u>comprised</u> four major themes.

As you can see from the last example, the whole (*speech*) comprises the parts (*themes*). A whole is never *comprised of* the parts. That would be the same as saying "The whole is included of its parts." Another way of looking at *comprise* is to think of it as embracing something, as in

> The chief justice's opinion <u>comprised</u> issues of privacy, false light and appropriation.

With all this said, it must be added that *comprise* is not a word we would use more than occasionally. Sometimes it just doesn't sound right!

compound modifiers These are two adjectives or an adverb joined with an adjective to modify a noun. Often a hyphen is needed to "join" these modifiers to make the meaning clear:

> mud-covered boat
> well-intentioned meaning
> hard-driving perfectionist

Veteran journalist James J. Kilpatrick spotted this advertisement in a Midwestern newspaper; its lack of hyphens made it read like a news report of an industrial accident:

> "Chef cut self basting turkeys"
> (Of course the ad was trying to sell chef-cut, self-basting turkeys.)

Modifiers do not require a hyphen if they are preceded by *very* or an *-ly* adverb. These adverbs obviously modify what follows, and there is no mistaking their connection.

> highly acclaimed production

very enthusiastic student

Don't string too many modifiers together in the name of description and economy. You'll simply get clutter.

conjunction This part of speech is a "joiner." It links words, phrases and clauses; if used properly, the conjunction provides both logic and rhythm to a sentence. Note, for example, how the conjunction *and* provides a nice sense of parallelism or equality to a clause:

> The border guard quickly stamped the passport <u>and</u> cheerfully directed the passenger to the nearest town.

But (a great conjunction—it provides a contrast or shows a lack of unity) note how the conjunction *and* can be improperly used when it links obviously unequal or unrhythmic elements in a sentence:

> She lost her fortune today on the stock market, <u>and</u> now she is heading to the gym.

This disjointed construction shows that conjunctions can't link everything effectively. Also see *as if/like* and p. 36.

conjunctive adverb Words like *however, therefore* and *nevertheless* may look like good linking constructions, but they really are adverbs. The use of a semicolon with conjunctive adverbs and the ability to move words like *therefore* around a sentence are good clues as to the real roles of these words. For example:

> The bids are well below the required minimum; <u>therefore,</u> I must cancel this auction.

Therefore is not a strong enough linking device, so a semicolon must be used to link the clauses. See p. 106.

continual/continuous *Continual* means "repeated or intermittent," and *continuous* means "unbroken."

> Must I suffer these <u>continual</u> interruptions?
> The delirious legionnaire saw a <u>continuous</u> line of canteens stretched across the barren horizon.

convince/persuade If you think these words are identical in meaning, we're just going to have to persuade you that they're not. We'll do that until you're convinced! To begin with, people do not *convince* others of anything; that action is called *persuasion*.

> The committee <u>persuaded</u> her to run for re-election.

To be *convinced* is to exist in a state in which one feels secure in a decision or a principle. It is always an adjective, not a verb.

> She is <u>convinced</u> she can win another term.

If a person attempts to persuade another and is successful, the first person is considered as persuasive. Obviously the argument has been convincing. The process is to persuade; the hoped-for result is to be convinced. Got that now? You cannot be convinced to do anything. You can be convinced that something is right or convinced of its correctness. Convinced? Or do you need to be persuaded?

dangling modifiers   A modifier dangles when it does not directly modify anything in the sentence. For example:

> <u>Facing indictment for income tax evasion,</u> the city council rescinded his appointment.

The participial phrase *facing indictment for income tax evasion* has nothing to modify. The first referent we see is *council*. It stretches both imagination and credulity to think the entire city council is under indictment. The only other possible referent is *appointment*, but this makes no sense. Poor sentence construction has buried the true referent—the person who is facing indictment. The sentence needs to be rewritten:

> <u>Facing indictment for income tax evasion,</u> <u>Smith</u> was ousted by the city council.

The participial phrase now has a referent, *Smith.*

Dangling modifiers most often occur at the beginnings of sentences. Although they tend to be *verbals* (participial phrases, gerund phrases and infinitive phrases), appositives, clauses and simple adjectives can dangle as well. The test is whether the person or thing being modified by the word, phrase or clause is in the sentence. Dangling modifiers destroy logical, coherent thought. Rewrite or revise the sentence to include the missing referent. See p. 142.

dash   An enticing piece of punctuation because of its informality, directness and drama, the dash (—) is often used excessively and incorrectly. Media writers should consider routinely using commas, colons and parentheses and saving dashes for special occasions. The two main uses of the dash in media writing are:

1. to create drama and emphasis at the end of a sentence

The film was beautifully photographed, superbly acted, expertly directed—and boring.

2. to clearly set off a long clause or phrase that adds information to the main clause

DA–DE

"Howard the Duck"—golden boy George Lucas' one and only mistake—was a box office bomb.

Use dashes for abrupt breaks and added emphasis. Remember that excessive use robs the dash of its power.

data and other foreign plurals Many English words have their roots in Latin; some are derived from Greek. Some of these words conform to singular-plural rules unlike our own. *Data, media* and *alumni* are commonly used Latin plurals. If you mean a single piece of information, use *datum* (although that would admittedly be rare). Magazines are one *medium;* radio and TV are broadcast *media.* The word *alumni* presents further complications: A group of men and women who have graduated from a school are *alumni;* one male graduate is an *alumnus;* one female grad is an *alumna.* And to be perfectly correct, a group of female grads would be *alumnae.* The Greek words *criteria* and *phenomena* are plural. Their singulars are *criterion* and *phenomenon.*

Data can be a difficult word in subject-verb agreement. It almost always is considered a unit, even though its form is plural. In this case, it is considered a collective noun and should take a singular verb:

Your data is invalid. (unit)

However, if the sense of data is individual items, use a plural verb:

The data were collected from seven tracking sites. (individual items)

dependent clause Although it contains both a predicate and a subject, a *dependent clause* does not express a complete thought and cannot stand alone as a sentence. Dependent clauses rely on main clauses for their completion.

Because the tax levy failed (dependent clause)
Because the tax levy failed, (dependent clause)
the county parks will be closed this summer. (independent clause)

Recognizing dependent clauses will help you to (1) avoid fragments (treating dependent clauses as if they were complete sentences) and (2) vary sentence structure. Place the dependent clause in front, in the middle or at the end of the main clause to vary sentence structure. See p. 44.

DI

different from/different than For those who take comfort from edicts, here's one: Use *different from* and you will never be wrong. If this leaves you wondering why *different than* exists, join the ranks of confused and contentious grammarians who have been arguing this point for years. Unless you're interested in delving into the nether regions of structural linguistics or semantic compatibility, consider using *different than* only when it introduces a *condensed clause* (a clause that omits certain words without loss of clarity).

Open meeting laws are different in Illinois than (they are) in Oregon. (condensed clause)

With a condensed clause, *different than* saves you from a wordier—but nonetheless grammatical—construction like *from that/those which*. To avoid clutter and clumsiness, you may want to use *different than*. In general, however, play it safe with *different from*. So the previous example would read

Open meeting laws in Oregon are different from those in Illinois.

differ from/differ with Politicians who *differ from* (are unlike) others may not necessarily *differ with* (disagree with) each other. Although these phrases express contrast, they are not interchangeable. When you mean two items are dissimilar, use *differ from*. When you mean items are in conflict, use *differ with*.

The subdivision homes did not differ from each other.
The housing developers differed with the zoning board.

discreet/discrete Yes, it's true—both of these words are adjectives, and both are pronounced the same. But they do have discrete meanings! *Discreet* means prudent or careful, especially about keeping confidences, as in this sentence:

The butler may have been stuffy, but he certainly was discreet.

Discrete means distinct or separate, as in this sentence:

Negotiators consider "outsourcing" a discrete issue in contract talks.

disinterested/uninterested A *disinterested* (impartial) observer may be *uninterested* (lack interest) in the situation, but the words are not synonymous.

drug A drug is any substance used as medicine in the treatment of a disease. Headline writers have made this word synonymous with *narcotics*, a particular group of sense-dulling, usually addictive drugs. All narcotics are drugs; all drugs are not narcotics. Be precise when using these words. To avoid confusion (and the possibility of libel), use *medicine* when referring to a substance used to treat a disease or an injury.

DR–EL

each/either/neither When used as subjects, these three pronouns always take singular verbs.

> <u>Each is</u> responsible for his or her own equipment.
> <u>Neither</u> of the defendants <u>was</u> found guilty.

When these words are used as adjectives, the nouns they modify always take a singular verb.

> <u>Either</u> answer <u>is</u> correct.
> <u>Neither</u> candidate <u>speaks</u> to the issues.

either ... or neither ... nor Called *correlative conjunctions,* these word pairs (along with *both ... and, not so ... as, not only ... but also*) should connect similar grammatical elements in parallel form.

> He can either pay the back taxes or a jail sentence might be imposed. (weak, lacks parallel structure)
> He can either pay the back taxes or risk a jail sentence. (improved, parallel)

Correlative conjunctions also pose agreement problems. When a compound subject is linked by a correlative conjunction, the subject closest to the verb determines the number of the verb.

> Neither the legislator <u>nor her aides were</u> available for comment.

When the subject closest to the verb is singular, you must use a singular verb. The construction is grammatical but sometimes graceless:

> Neither the aides <u>nor the legislator was</u> available for comment.

Avoid awkwardness by placing the plural subject next to the verb. See p. 62.

elicit/illicit These two words may sound alike, but the similarity stops there. *Elicit,* a verb, means "to bring out" or "draw forth." *Illicit,* an adjective, means "illegal" or "unlawful."

> His <u>illicit</u> behavior <u>elicited</u> strong community reaction.

eminent/imminent These are both adjectives, but they describe very different qualities. *Eminent* means distinguished or prominent, as in

Memorial services are pending for the <u>eminent</u> professor.

Imminent means "about to occur" or impending, as in

The Internet company is facing an <u>imminent</u> takeover.

Spelling aficionados take note: There is one *m* in *eminent,* two in *imminent.* Don't ask us why!

enormity/enormousness Be wary of this pair. These words are not synonymous. *Enormity* means "wickedness." *Enormousness* refers to "size."

The <u>enormity</u> of his deception was not discovered for years.
The <u>enormousness</u> and complexity of the problem staggered even the greatest political thinkers.

exclamation point Expressing strong emotion or surprise, the exclamation point (!) is rarely used in journalistic writing. Its use is almost always limited to direct quotations. Remember to place the exclamation point inside the quotation marks.

"I'll kill you when this is over!" the witness screamed at the prosecutor.

farther/further One of these years, you probably won't have to worry about this bothersome duo. *Farther,* say grammarians, is on the way out. But language often changes slowly, and the distinction between these two words will be with us for a while. Use *farther* to express physical distance; use *further* when referring to "degree, time or quantity."

The commission recommended extending the boundaries <u>farther</u> to the south.
The commission will discuss the boundary issue <u>further</u>.

feel Save this overused word to refer to the tactile or emotional; do not use it as a synonym for *think* or *believe.*

fewer/less This is a much-abused pair, but the distinctions are simple: When you refer to a number of individual items, *fewer* is your choice; when you refer to a bulk, amount, sum, period of time or concept, use *less.*

<u>Fewer</u> doctors result in <u>less</u> medical care.
At Data Corporation, <u>fewer</u> than 10 employees make <u>less</u> than $50,000 a year.

In the latter example, we are not talking about individual dollars but a sum (amount) of money.

fragments An unfinished piece of a sentence, a fragment may be a single word, a phrase or a dependent clause. It may lack a subject, a predicate, a complete thought or any combination of the three. Whatever form it takes, whatever element it lacks, a fragment is not a grammatical sentence and should not stand alone. Fragments can be rewritten to include subject, predicate and complete thought; incorporated into complete sentences; or attached to main clauses. See pp. 46–47 and the *sentence* entry.

FR–GE

Now you know the rule. Here's the loophole: Fragments, when used purposefully by skillful writers, constitute a stylistic technique. With their clipped, punchy beat, fragments can create excitement and grab reader attention. But this special stylistic device must be appropriate to both subject and medium and should be used sparingly.

gender-specific references (*he/she*) Language reflects culture and beliefs. When a society changes, we believe language ought to keep pace. We are speaking not of faddish words or slang expressions but of the way language treats people. The language in the following sentences is no longer an accurate reflection of our society:

A nurse ought to be attentive to her patients.
A state legislator has a responsibility to his constituents.

In these sentences we see outdated gender stereotypes—nurses are female, legislators are male. From a grammatical point of view, the problem is choosing a referent (*she, he, him, her, his, hers*) that reflects reality rather than presuming maleness or femaleness of a neuter noun. Because the singular neuter pronoun (*it, its*) cannot refer to a person, we have two grammatical options if we want to avoid sexual stereotyping:

1. Use both the masculine and the feminine pronoun when referencing a noun that could refer to either sex.

   A nurse ought to be attentive to his or her patients.

2. Change the neuter noun to the plural and use plural neuter pronouns (*they, them, their*).

   State legislators have a responsibility to their constituents.

In your effort to treat both sexes fairly in language, don't fall prey to "political" solutions that accept errors in agreement. The following sentence from an organization's newsletter employs a singular subject, singular verb and plural possessive pronoun:

<u>Everybody deserves</u> to make it on <u>their</u> own.

This may be well-intentioned, but it does not advance the cause of non-sexist language; it abuses correct language. Two solutions are obvious:

Everybody deserves to make it on his or her own.
All people deserve to make it on their own.

(See Chapter 11.)

hanged/hung   The verb *hang* is conjugated differently depending on the object of the hanging. The conjugation *hang, hung, hung* refers to objects.

The portrait <u>hung</u> in the museum foyer.

The conjugation *hang, hanged, hanged* refers to people (executions or suicides).

He <u>hanged</u> himself in his prison cell.

historic/historical   These are not synonymous terms. *Historic* means that something has achieved a place in history, as in

The treaty marks an <u>historic</u> moment in relations between preser-vationists and whalers. (Note the use of the article *an* before *historic*; sound controls this choice in our opinion, though there is considerable dispute over the *a/an* choice.)

Historical means "of or relating to history," as in

Randy enjoys reading <u>historical</u> novels.

hopefully   Possibly the single most abused word in our language, *hopefully* means "with hope." It describes how a subject feels (*hopeful*). Therefore, this sentence would be correct:

<u>Hopefully,</u> he opened the mailbox looking for the check.

Hopefully—regardless of what you may hear or read—does not mean "it is hoped that." Therefore, the following sentence is incorrect:

Hopefully, the check will arrive.

The check is not "hopeful." *Hopefully* does not describe anything in the preceding sentence. It is, in fact, a dangling modifier. People have so thoroughly abused *hopefully* in conversational language (making it synonymous with "it is hoped") that the abuse is now part of our written language. For correctness, precision and clarity, respect the real meaning of the word. If you mean "it is hoped," write that.

hyphen   A typographical bridge that links words, the hyphen (-) has three uses in media writing:

HY–IF

1. It joins compound modifiers unless one of the modifiers is *very* or an *-ly* adverb. Compound modifiers are two or more adjectives or adverbs that do not separately describe the word they modify.

   a <u>well-mannered</u> child (hyphen needed)
   the <u>newly elected</u> senator (*-ly* adverb, no hyphen needed)

2. It links certain prefixes to the words that follow. It's best to check a dictionary or stylebook on this rule because exceptions abound. One basic guideline is this: If the prefix ends in a vowel and the next word begins with the same vowel, hyphenate (except *cooperate* and *coordinate*).

3. It links words when a preposition is omitted.

   score of 5-3 (preposition *to* omitted)
   June-August profits (preposition *through* omitted)

See pp. 114–116.

-ics words   Words ending with the Greek suffix *-ics* (*athletics, politics, graphics, acoustics, tactics,* etc.) often present agreement problems. Although the final *s* makes these words look plural, they can be either singular or plural depending on meaning. If the word refers to "a science, art or general field of study," it is treated as singular and takes a singular verb. If the word refers to "the act, practices or activities" of the field, it takes a plural verb.

   Politics <u>is</u> a challenging career. (the field of politics, singular)
   His politics <u>change</u> every year. (the practice of politics, plural)

Some *-ics* words do not carry both meanings. *Hysterics,* for example, always takes the plural because it always refers to "acts and practices."

if I were   This common subjunctive mood construction is often mistakenly written, "If I was." But the subjunctive mood, which is used to express a nonexistent, hypothetical or improbable condition, influences the form of the verb. *Were* is the subjunctive form of the verb *to be.* The following sentences are grammatically correct:

If <u>she were</u> president, we would have a balanced budget.
If the housing <u>industry were</u> to collapse, the local economy would soon follow.

if/whether   These conjunctions are not interchangeable. *If* means "in the event that," "granting that," "on the condition that." It is often used to introduce a *subjunctive clause* (a clause that expresses a nonexistent, hypothetical or improbable condition).

<u>If</u> Smith loses, the Democrats will have a majority. (in the event that)
<u>If</u> the volcano were to erupt again, hundreds would have to be evacuated. (hypothetical condition)

Whether means "if it is so that," "if it happens that" or "in case." It is generally used to introduce a possibility.

She asked <u>whether</u> the evidence was admissible. (if it is so)
<u>Whether</u> he wins or loses, this will be his last campaign. (introduces a set of possibilities)

For the sake of precision and conciseness, use *whether,* not *whether or not.* The *or not* is implied. To state it is redundant.

<u>Whether [or not]</u> the schools stay open depends on the fate of the budget levy.

impact   Robbed of its power by overuse, *impact* means a "collision" or a "violent or forceful striking together." Unfortunately, writers use *impact* when they really mean something much calmer such as *effect* or *influence.*

When her car hit the guard rail, the <u>impact</u> caused the vehicle to jackknife. (correct)
No one knows what <u>impact</u> the report will have on future development. (a misuse—better to use effect or influence)

Impact has also fallen prey to jargon mongers who now incorrectly employ it as a verb ("The televised debates *impacted* the election") or an adjective ("federally *impacted* areas"). The only thing that can be impacted is a tooth, and that's unpleasant enough.

imply/infer   Often confused, these verbs are not interchangeable. *Imply* means "to suggest or hint." *Infer* means "to deduce or conclude from facts or evidence."

IF–IM

When he <u>implied</u> Smith was guilty, the jury <u>inferred</u> he had an ax to grind.

indefinite pronouns   Because indefinite pronouns don't always specify number (*anyone, everyone, few, some*), they can cause agreement problems. Here are a few rules to follow:

- When used as subjects, *each, either, anyone, everyone, much, no one, nothing* and *someone* always take a singular verb.

- Acting as subjects, *both, few, many* and *several* always take a plural verb.

- Pronouns such as *any, none* and *some* take singular verbs when they refer to "a unit or general quantity." If they refer to "amount or individuals," they take a plural verb.

    <u>Some</u> of the construction <u>was</u> delayed (general quantity) because <u>some</u> of the workers <u>were</u> on strike. (individuals)

See p. 62–63.

independent clause   Also known as the *principal* or *main clause,* an independent clause contains a subject, predicate and complete thought. When it stands alone as a grammatically complete sentence, it is called a *simple sentence.* Two independent clauses linked by a coordinating conjunction make a compound sentence. See pp. 43–44.

-ing endings   A common suffix, *-ing* can be added to a verb to create the present progressive form ("She is running for office") or a verbal ("Running for office requires stamina"). It can also be added to a noun, creating a verbal that gives the noun a sense of action. *Parenting* is the action of being a *parent* (and follows the linguistic tradition of *mother/mothering*).

Although *-inging* a noun can be a useful device that creates new words with distinct meanings, it can also be unnecessarily trendy. Language should change in response to culture and not merely for the sake of change. For example,

Gifting is a holiday tradition

is an ugly, awkward construction. Use new *-ing* words sparingly and only when they capture a unique meaning without damaging the rhythm and sound of the language.

IN

in/into These prepositions are not interchangeable. *In* denotes location or position. *Into* indicates motion.

>The judge was <u>in</u> the courtroom. (location, position)
>The next witness walked <u>into</u> the courtroom. (movement)

Regardless of current slang, *into* should never be used as a substitute for "involved with" or "interested in." This colloquial use is not only sloppy but also weak and ambiguous.

>For the past year, she's been into swimming. (ambiguous slang)
>She's been swimming a mile a day for the past year. (improved)

initiate/instigate At our own instigation, we have initiated an investigation of this troublesome pair. It is not correct to write, for example,

>He <u>instigated</u> the first tofu sculpture contest

when you mean that this deluded artist began or originated the contest. Instead, he *initiated* (began) it. This would be a proper use of *instigate:*

>At great personal expense, he <u>instigated</u> an investigation of the Baldness Is Natural Foundation.

In this case, he did not begin the investigation—he pressed for it.

insure/ensure/assure Please he assured: These words are different! If you limit the meaning of *insure* to activities of insurance companies, you'll do fine.

>Continental refused to <u>insure</u> him because of his pre-existing medical condition.

Ensure, on the other hand, means (in a noninsurance sense) "to guarantee" or "to provide something," as in:

>She promised to do all she could to <u>ensure</u> our safety.

What about *assure?* If used properly, this verb speaks directly to a person, to give him or her confidence in a promise:

>She <u>assured</u> them that they would be safe.

Insure/ensure/assure are further examples of a dictionary's failure to show truly distinct meanings for truly different words.

invoke/evoke Probably because both words contain *-voke* from the Latin root *vocare* ("to call"), these very different words are often treated as interchangeable. *Invoke* means "to appeal to or call forth earnestly." *Evoke* means "to produce or elicit" (a reaction, a response) or "to reawaken" (memories, for example).

When the speaker <u>invoked</u> God, he <u>evoked</u> a strong reaction from the audience of atheists.

irregardless Banish this word from your vocabulary. *Regardless,* which means "without regard for" or "unmindful of" is the word you're after. The *-less* suffix creates the negative meaning. When you mistakenly add the *-ir* prefix, you create a double negative.

IR–KI

its/it's *Its* is the possessive form of the neuter pronoun *it.* Do not confuse this with *it's,* which is a contraction for *it is* or *it has.*

The committee reached <u>its</u> decision yesterday. (neuter possessive)
"<u>It's</u> going to be a close vote," said Smith. (contraction for *it is*)

Use *it* or *its*—not *she* or *her*—when referring to nations or ships.

Mexico is carefully patrolling <u>its</u> borders.
The S. S. <u>France</u> made <u>its</u> first voyage more than 20 years ago.

-ize words A useful suffix, *-ize* has been employed since the time of the ancient Greeks to change nouns into verbs (*final/finalize, burglar/ burglarize*). But the *-ization* of words has now reached epidemic proportions. We've been alarmed at the growing use of *incentivize,* for example. Writers interested in the clarity, precision and beauty of language need to take precautions. Tacking *-ize* onto nouns often creates useless, awkward and stodgy words.

The commander announced a new plan to <u>soldierize</u> the troops.
The agency may <u>permanentize</u> its position by <u>routinizing</u> its procedures.

"Verbizing" nouns is dangerous business. The result is often tongue-twisting, bureaucratic-sounding clutter. Before you use an *-ize* word, check your dictionary. Make sure the word has a unique meaning, and pay attention to sound. See p. 135.

kind of/sort of Conversationally we use *kind of* and *sort of* to mean "rather" or "somewhat":

It's <u>kind of</u> (a somewhat) cloudy today.
I'm <u>sort of</u> (rather) tired.

But casual usage and clear, precise written language are often two different things. Restrict your use of *kind of* and *sort of* to mean "a species or subcategory of," as in:

> This is the <u>kind of</u> development Boomtown needs.

In many cases you can eliminate the problems posed by *kind of* and *sort of* by avoiding the words themselves. Often these phrases merely take up space without adding meaning.

lay/lie *Lay,* a transitive verb, always requires a direct object. *Lie,* an intransitive verb, never takes a direct object.

> Before <u>lying</u> down, she <u>laid</u> the book on the table.
> (no direct object) (direct object)

Be careful not to confuse *lie* and *lay* in the past tense. The past tense of *lie* is *lay;* the past tense of *lay* is *laid.*

> lie, lay, lain, lying
> lay, laid, lain, laying

See pp. 16–17.

lend/loan Because *lend* has a longer history as a verb, many language experts prefer it to *loan* in written usage. But *loan,* originally a noun, has also come to mean "to lend" as a verb, and the distinction between the two words is fading. In spoken language, the distinction is almost nonexistent. Rather than worry about the differing niceties observed by various media organizations or editors, play it safe: Use *lend* as a verb and *loan* as a noun. The one exception currently favored by most experts is *loan* as a verb in financial contexts:

> The bank <u>loaned</u> the senator $1.5 million.

This would be an appropriate use of *lend:*

> Lee is angry because his roommate won't <u>lend</u> him the new "Jabba" CD.

less than/under Do not use *under* unless you mean "physically underneath." If you mean "a lesser quantity or amount," use *less than.*

> The county budget was <u>under</u> $80 million. (incorrect)
> The county budget was <u>less than</u> $80 million. (correct)

Also see the entries for *fewer/less* and *more than/over.*

linking verbs A linking verb connects a subject to an equivalent word in the sentence. That word—a predicate noun, a predicate pronoun or a predicate adjective—refers to the subject by either restating it or describing it. The principal linking verbs are *be, seem, become, appear, feel* and *look.*

> She <u>became</u> a best-selling novelist. (*Novelist,* a predicate noun, restates subject *she.*)
>
> It <u>is</u> he. (*He,* a predicate pronoun, restates the subject *it.*)
>
> He <u>feels</u> bad. (*Bad,* a predicate adjective, describes the subject *he.*)

Note that the predicate pronoun following a linking verb must be in the nominative case.

> It is <u>he</u>.

Not:

> It is <u>him</u>.

LI–LO

Remember that a modifier following a linking verb must be an adjective, not an adverb.

> He feels <u>bad</u>.

Not:

> He feels <u>badly</u>.

See the entry for *bad/badly* and pp. 17–18.

literal/figurative Considering these two words are opposites, it's both odd and interesting that writers sometimes mistakenly substitute one for another. *Literal* means "word for word" or "upholding the exact meaning of a word," as in:

> This is a <u>literal</u> translation of the book.

Figurative, on the other hand, means "not literal, metaphorical, based on figures of speech," as in:

> <u>Figuratively</u> speaking, she was on top of the world.

loath/loathe To begin with, *loath* is an adjective and *loathe* is a verb. *Loath* means "reluctant" or "hostile to," as in

> We are <u>loath</u> to accept your explanation of the accident.

Loathe means "to detest" or "to show great disgust or hate for," as in

> I <u>loathe</u> classes where instructors drone on like leaf blowers.

may/might Time to split those proverbial hairs! Both of these verbs indicate possibility, as in "I may go to Uganda next month," but usage "classicists" tell us that *may* indicates a stronger possibility than *might*. More informal usage suggests that *might* is less stilted than *may*. So what to do? Stick with *may* unless the possibilities for action are extremely remote, as in

> I <u>might</u> as well be the man in the moon.

MA–MI

median/average (mean) Election results, political polls, budgets, research findings—so much of today's reporting depends on numbers and statistics that journalists ought to understand at least a few basic terms. *Median* is the middle value in a distribution of items, the point at which half of the items are above and half below. *Average* is the sum of a group of items divided by the number of items in the group. *Mean* is statisticians' talk for average. Statistically, average and mean are virtually synonymous.

> Number of years spent on death row by prisoners of state X:
>
> | | | |
> |---|---|---|
> | Prisoner A 18 | Prisoner D 10 | Prisoner G 6 |
> | Prisoner B 14 | Prisoner E 7 | Prisoner H 6 |
> | Prisoner C 10 | Prisoner F 6 | Prisoner I 4 |

The *median* years spent on death row is 7; that is, half of the prisoners spent more than 7 years in jail, half spent less. The *average* (or *mean*) number of years spent on death row is 9; it is the sum of all the years divided by the number of people.

misplaced modifiers A misplaced modifier is a single word, phrase or clause that does not clearly and logically point to what it is supposed to modify. Be meticulous in your placement of modifiers. Place them next to, or as close as possible to, the word or words they describe. Misplacement not only causes confusion but also can change the meaning of a sentence.

> The committee <u>almost</u> defeated every budget item. (The adverb *almost* modifies *defeated*.)
> The committee defeated <u>almost</u> every budget item. (*Almost* modified *every*, which modifies *budget item*.)

more than/over Like *less than* and *under,* these words are not interchangeable. Do not use *over* unless you are referring to a spatial relationship. For figures and amounts, the correct phrase is *more than.*

More than 400 fighter planes flew bombing missions over the gulf.

none This troublesome indefinite pronoun often causes agreement problems. Use a singular verb when *none* means "no one or not one." When *none* means "no two, no amount or no number," use a plural verb. The singular/plural choice depends on the meaning of the sentence.

None ("not one") of the reporters was admitted to the courtroom.
None ("no amount") of the taxes were paid.

See the entry for *indefinite pronouns* and pp. 62–63.

MO-NU

noun Perhaps the hardest-working part of speech, the noun truly frames a sentence, from subject to object. However, one of its more confusing roles is that of a *gerund,* an *-ing* word that also can serve as subject or object, as in

Eating all those hot dogs has ruined my appetite for cheesecake.

Note the singular verb *has ruined* in this construction; *eating,* a noun disguised as a gerund, is the true, singular subject. See also *verbals* and p. 57.

numerals Your organization may have specific style rules concerning numerals. Check first. In the absence of other guidelines, follow these rules:

1. Spell out whole numbers below 10: three, seven.

2. Use figures for 10 and above: 14, 305.

3. Spell out fractions less than one: two-thirds, three-quarters.

4. Spell out *first* through *ninth* when they indicate a sequence: She was first in line; the Ninth Amendment. Use figures for 10th and above.

5. Spell out numerals at the beginning of a sentence. The only exception is a calendar-year date.

These are general rules. Your organization may have special guidelines for ages, percentages, fractions, election returns, monetary units, dimensions, temperatures or other special cases. The Associated Press Stylebook is a good reference.

occur/take place Although one of the secondary definitions for *occur* is "to take place," contemporary journalistic use favors this distinction: *Occur* refers to "all accidental or unscheduled events"; *take place* refers to "a planned event."

> The power outage <u>occurred</u> at approximately 3 p.m.
> Opening ceremonies will <u>take place</u> tomorrow afternoon at 2.

off of Be wary of prepositions that enjoy one another's company. You may be practicing grammatical "featherbedding"—having two do the job of one. *Off of* is one of those redundant, bulky constructions. *Off,* all by its lonesome, suffices.

> Get <u>off (of)</u> my back!
> Driscoll walked <u>off (of)</u> the stage and never performed again.

OC–ON

We are also suspicious of the phrase *across from.* However, the insertion of an object between these two words solves the awkwardness of the construction.

> The appliance store is <u>across from</u> the pharmacy.
> The appliance store is <u>across the street from</u> the pharmacy.

The addition of two words does not hurt the conciseness of the sentence. It certainly helps its clarity.

one of the/the only one of the Making a verb agree in number with its subject is not difficult—once you identify the proper subject. When the subject is a pronoun (*who* or *that,* for example) that refers to a noun elsewhere in the sentence, the task is somewhat challenging. Subject-verb agreement then depends on determining the correct antecedent. For *one of the/only one of the,* follow these rules:

1. In *one of the* constructions the relative pronoun refers to the object of the preposition of the main clause, not the subject.

> Easter is <u>one</u> of the best <u>ballplayers</u> who <u>have</u> played
>   (subj.)   (obj. of prep.) (pron.) (verb)
> the game in the last 50 years. (If you examine this sentence, you will see that *Easter* is not the only ball-player who has played the game in 50 years. We are talking about *many players* who *have* played the game in that period. We are saying that Easter is included in that group.)

2. In *the only one of the* constructions the relative pronoun refers to the subject of the main clause.

Jennings is the only one of the candidates who has opposed the
(subj.)   (pron.)   (verb)
nuclear freeze referendum. (There were no other candidates who opposed this referendum. The antecedent clearly is *Jennings*.)

See pp. 64–65.

parallel structure When you place like ideas in like grammatical patterns, you create parallel structure. This consistency among elements gives order to your writing and helps make the message clear. Parallelism also creates balance, symmetry—and sometimes rhythm—in a sentence. Common errors in parallelism include mixing elements in a series, mixing verbals and switching voice. See pp. 67–69.

parentheses Media writers use parentheses sparingly in their writing because the reason for their use—to provide additional information or an aside for the sentence—is generally contrary to brief, crisp writing. For those rare occasions when you do use them, here is a simple rule concerning punctuation: Put the period inside the parentheses only if the parenthetical material is a complete sentence and can stand independently of the preceding sentence.

PA-PE

Don't fry onions in bacon grease. (You'll be asking for trouble.)

If these conditions are not met, the period goes outside.

The funeral-goers chanted "Vaya con Dios" (Go with God).

See pp. 117–118.

passive voice An odd, generally ineffective and quite deceptive construction in which the subject of the sentence is actually the recipient of the verb's action, it also creates unnecessary wordiness. Note the difference in directness and conciseness between these two examples:

The ultimatum was delivered by an angry band of protestors. (passive)
An angry band of protestors delivered the ultimatum. (active)

See Chapter 6.

people/persons Some contend that a group is referred to as *people* but individuals are *persons*. We find it difficult to create a scale for acceptable use of *persons* (three? six?) and to set a cutoff point (seven people?), so it seems only reasonable to avoid the plural *persons*. Why do seven persons somehow have separate identities, but 28 people do not? After many years of using *persons,* the Associated Press Stylebook now agrees with us. Save yourself the headache! There are more pressing decisions in life.

If you are referring to "an individual," you are referring to a *person*.

Ohman thought the president was a kind <u>person</u> but an inept leader.

If you are referring to "more than one," you are referring to *people*.

<u>Four thousand people</u> demonstrated at the Capitol today in opposition to welfare cuts.

per This Latin preposition, meaning "through, by, by means of," is used today only when scientific or technical writing calls for it or when the Latin phrase associated with it fits the context of the story. Whereas we still use terms such as *miles per gallon, per capita expenditures* and *percent*, we do not say *$40 per day* or *$18,000 per year*. If you can replace *per* with the indefinite article *a* or *an* without awkwardness, do it.

possessives Chapter 5 discusses in detail the formation of possessives. One point about them, however, deserves emphasis: Possessives of personal pronouns are not the same as contractions.

Remember that the personal pronoun possessives (*my, mine, our, ours, your, yours, his, her, hers, its, their, theirs*) do not require an apostrophe. See p. 78–80 and the entry for *its/it's*.

preposition This is a handy part of speech that links phrases and neatly ties a sentence into a coherent package, as in

The burglar was hiding <u>behind</u> the door. (The preposition <u>behind</u> begins the prepositional phrase.)

Although a preposition can occasionally introduce a clause, it almost always leads a phrase. When that phrase contains a pronoun, that pronoun must stay in the objective case, as in

Deadlines are an energizer <u>for us writers</u>.

Writers sometimes use prepositions excessively, burdening a sentence with a series, as in

Dr. Demento followed his victim <u>through</u> the French doors <u>next to</u> the solarium, <u>with</u> the evil intent <u>of</u> murder <u>on</u> his mind.

Let prepositions enhance a sentence—don't let them drain the power of its verb!

preventive/preventative Why in the world use *preventative?* It uses two extra letters and still means preventive! It's pretentious, that's why. Practice preventive language arts—avoid overweight words.

principal/principle   As a noun, *principal* means "someone who is first in rank or authority," such as the principal of a school. As an adjective, *principal* still means "first in rank or authority," such as the "principal reason for the levy's defeat." *Principle,* however, is only a noun. It means "a truth, doctrine or rule of conduct," such as "an uncompromising principle of honesty." Obviously, the only thing common to these two words is their sound.

prior to   Use *before. Prior to* is stuffy and falsely formal.

pronoun   It means, literally, "in place of a noun." Unlike nouns, pronouns change their form in the possessive (for example, *their* for *they*), which is why pronoun possessives don't need apostrophes (and that's why *it's* is not a pronoun!). Careless writers often position their pronouns indiscriminately, causing problems with antecedent identification, as in

> The Pentagon <u>briefers</u> tried to decipher the field reports for the <u>journalists,</u> but it was apparent that <u>they</u> were hopelessly confused.

Get the idea? If you are going to use a pronoun, be sure that the antecedent is properly identified. See pp. 64–65.

proved/proven   Current usage supports *proved* as the past participle of the verb *prove.*

> Coke has <u>proved</u> the merits of its ad campaign.

Proven, although cited by some dictionaries as an acceptable alternate for the past participle, is preferred in journalistic style as an adjective only.

> The Internet Dating Game is a <u>proven</u> success.

In a linking verb construction, then, you use *proven* if it takes the role of the predicate adjective:

> Coke's success is <u>proven.</u>
> (*Proven* is not part of the verb. It is an adjective that modifies *success.*)

quotation marks   One of the most common concerns about quotation marks is where to place other marks of punctuation. Here is a brief recap:

1. Periods and commas always go inside.

2. Question marks and exclamation marks go inside if they are part of the quoted material.

The most common error in quotation mark punctuation is in placement of the question mark. Two examples show the correct placement:

The senator asked the nervous lobbyist: "Can you honestly tell me that your baby food formula has never caused the death of a child in a Third World country?" (The question mark belongs inside because it is part of a quoted question.)

Have you seen all the toys modeled after "Rambo"? (The entire sentence is a question; the title is declarative.)

See Chapter 7 for more information on quotation marks and other marks of punctuation.

quotation/quote   *Quotation* is a noun. *Quote* is a verb. However, the twain meet in newsrooms, where *quote* is often used as a noun. ("Get me some good quotes for this piece. It's dying of boredom.") Journalists are economical souls. That's why the verb *quote* has been changed to suit the purposes of the secret language of the newsroom. We urge you to keep the use there. In any writing for the noninitiated public, remember to quote only the good quotations.

ravage/ravish   To *ravage* is to destroy or ruin.

A string of tornadoes <u>ravaged</u> the small Illinois town of Conant.

To *ravish* is to carry away forcibly or to rape.

The conquering army <u>ravished</u> the Trojan women.

rebut/refute   It's easier to rebut a statement than to refute it. When you *rebut* a statement, you contradict it or deny it. But that doesn't mean you have done so successfully. When you *refute* a statement, you conclusively prove that you are correct. Use *refute* in your newswriting only if there is a consensus that the denial has been successful. Don't make the judgment on your own.

reluctant/reticent   People who are reluctant to do something are not necessarily reticent. A *reluctant* person is unwilling to do something.

At first, Smith was <u>reluctant</u> to enter the presidential race.

If a person is unwilling to speak readily or is uncommonly reserved, we generally describe that person as *reticent*.

The professor has instituted a class for <u>reticent</u> speakers.

renown/renowned Often confused, these two words are different parts of speech. *Renown,* the noun, means "fame or eminence." *Renowned,* the adjective, means "famous or celebrated."

> Renowned scientist and Nobel laureate Linus Pauling won renown for his ground-breaking work in chemistry.

restrictive/nonrestrictive These high-sounding terms refer to the role of phrases and clauses in a sentence. A *restrictive clause* is an essential clause that helps define the meaning of a sentence. Identifying this type of clause helps you in two ways:

1. The restrictive clause does not need to be set off by commas.

2. In a choice between *that* and *which, that* is always the correct pronoun subject or object.

> The poll that the senator commissioned has not gone well for her.
> (The restrictive clause is underlined; without it, the sentence lacks definition.)

A *nonrestrictive clause* is not essential to the context of the sentence. It must be set off by commas, and you use *which* instead of *that* when the choice has to be made.

RE-SA

> Political polls, which are a staple of modern campaigning, are an important key to party fund raising. (The nonrestrictive clause is underlined; the sentence can be understood without it.)

run-on sentence Like the boorish practical joker, it doesn't know when to stop. The run-on may actually be several sentences rolled into one and molded into an amalgam of confusion because of improper punctuation.

> Picket lines went up for a fourth straight day, nurses vowed to continue to honor them until contract talks resume.

Use of a semicolon instead of a comma or the insertion of the conjunction *and* after the comma would have corrected this fault. See also the entry for *comma splice* and pp. 47–49.

said Don't overlook the use of this valuable verb when quoting someone. Searching for variety, writers sometimes reach out for *stated, uttered, elucidated, declared* or what have you. Describing the speaker and his or her delivery is more important than poring over a thesaurus to find a verb that is better off in a game of Scrabble than in journalistic writing. Also, don't overlook the value of quoting someone in the present tense.

semicolon   This important tool will help you avoid the run-on sentence. When two independent clauses are in one sentence and are not separated by a conjunction such as *or, but* or *and,* they must be separated by a semicolon:

> He is not your ordinary movie star; he is already a legendary figure in cinema.

When two independent clauses are joined by a conjunctive adverb such as *however, nevertheless* or *therefore,* a semicolon also is needed:

> I can't speak for this faculty; however, I am opposed to any reduction in our humanities curriculum.

sentence   A sentence is one or more independent clauses that present a complete thought. Writers do awful things to sentences: They run one into another, they clutter them with unnecessary punctuation, and sometimes they forget to put a verb in one but still call it a sentence,

> Like this.

SE

Sentences are the framework for all written thoughts. Good writers subordinate other clauses and phrases within them and logically arrange their sentences into cohesive, nicely moving paragraphs. A good sentence is an enlightenment, a forceful directive, an amusing bit of play. But it is always well-contained; its thought is always complete. See Chapter 3.

set/sit   Normally the verb *set* requires an object:

> Please <u>set</u> the <u>package</u> on the table.

Sit, however, never takes an object:

> Won't you please <u>sit</u> down?

sex and gender   Historically *gender* has meant the indication of male or female in our words—most prominently in our personal pronouns (*he, she, him, her,* etc.). However, contemporary usage seems to favor *gender* over *sex* in discussing differences based on sex, as in

> Firefighter is acceptable as a <u>gender</u>-neutral term.

This does not seem to apply, however, in the all-too-common terms *sex discrimination* or *sexual harrasment,* but stay tuned—change is in the wind.

since/because These words are not synonymous. *Since* is best used when it denotes a period of time, whether continuous or broken.

> It has been many years <u>since</u> we have had a balanced budget.

Because gives a reason or cause.

> We haven't had a balanced budget <u>because</u> the government can't control its spending.

Note that in most circumstances a comma is not needed before *because*.

so This is a weak conjunction when it means "with the result that." It isn't strong enough to coordinate two independent clauses in one sentence.

> Dr. Carolan couldn't decide whether Williams or Doerr should bat fourth, <u>so</u> he flipped a coin to speed his decision.

You will find that a rewrite is more direct and economical:

> Dr. Carolan flipped a coin to see whether Williams or Doerr would bat fourth.

SI–SP

Another choice—and more direct than the *so* solution—is

> Because Dr. Carolan couldn't decide whether Williams or Doerr should bat fourth, he flipped a coin. (Note also the choice of *whether* instead of *if* in these sentences.)

split constructions The split infinitive is a usual topic in grammar texts. However, the chief reason for objecting to the split infinitive—loss of clarity—is also the reason for avoiding unnecessary splits of a subject and a verb and of a verb and its complement. When writing these constructions, be aware of a loss of clarity when the split becomes awkward. Some examples:

> The Cubs pledged <u>to</u> before the end of the month <u>break</u> their losing streak. (A split infinitive—insertion of the two prepositional phrases between the two parts of the verb—causes confusion.)
> <u>Benson,</u> before switching to the Minolta line of equipment and commercially endorsing it, <u>used</u> "plate cameras" early in his career. (A split between subject and verb—although not unusual—is awkward when it causes the reader to lose track of the thought.)
> The prime minister reportedly <u>objected,</u> in a secret meeting with French diplomats held yesterday morning, to recent European <u>trade agreements</u>. (A split between the verb and its complement disturbs the natural flow by injecting lengthy explanatory material.)

Clarity and flow are the key issues. Obviously, strict adherence to a "no splits" policy can lead to unimaginative writing. See pp. 143–144.

than/then   *Than* is used as a conjunction of comparison, although some grammarians say it can be a preposition if the clause of comparison is understood. Rather than deal with all of that here, our point is that *then*—an adverb denoting time—is often confused with *than*. If you are comparing something, use *than*:

> No one is more aware of America's breakfast habits <u>than</u> the fast-food magnates.

Then, on the other hand, carries the sense of "soon afterward":

> First, we'll go to the art exhibit; <u>then</u> we'll try to get a table at that great Armenian restaurant. (Note that *then* cannot connect these two independent clauses on its own. A semicolon is needed.)

When *than* is used to introduce an implied clause of comparison, the pronoun that may follow is most likely in the nominative case:

> Tom is a lot smarter than <u>I</u> (am smart).

But some sentences won't permit this implied arrangement:

> There is not a more dedicated student than <u>him</u>. ("Than he is a student" would not make sense here.)

For more information on this, see pp. 75–76.

that/which/who   As the entry for *restrictive/nonrestrictive* says, *that* is used to restrict meaning and *which* is used to elaborate on it. These pronouns are used only in their particular types of clauses, but *who* can be used in both types when it refers to people or to things endowed by the writer with human qualities. Examples:

> Construction bonds <u>that</u> are issued by local governments generally carry tax-free interest. (restrictive meaning)
> Construction bonds, <u>which</u> can be a dependable tax shelter, carry different interest rates according to the credit standing of the local government. (nonrestrictive—gives explanation)
> The people <u>who</u> interrupted the demonstration were arrested. (restrictive—in this case, *that* would be inappropriate)
> Hollings, <u>who</u> is running for the State Senate seat from Culver City, charged this morning that the governor's office has been "grossly mismanaged." (nonrestrictive—explanatory material follows *who*)

TH

For a discussion of the selection of *who* and punctuation of these clauses, see pp. 28 and 100–102 and the entry for *restrictive/nonrestrictive.*

their/there/they're Although they sound alike, these words have different functions in a sentence. *Their* is the possessive form of the pronoun *they.* It should cause little problem.

> Their presentation is scheduled for 3 p.m. (*Their* modifies the noun *presentation.*)

When it begins a sentence, *there* is called an *expletive.* It is sometimes called a *false subject* because it doesn't help determine the number of the verb.

> There are only 26 shopping days until Christmas. (Note that *days,* not *there,* controls the number of the verb.)

They're is a contraction of *they* and *are,* used only informally when you want to combine subject and verb:

> "They're here," he said, looking out the window.

there are/there is Beginning a sentence with the expletive *there* is generally an indirect and ineffective way to communicate. It adds clutter, not meaning. When you have to use it, however, be aware that *there* is not the subject of the sentence and does not control the number of the verb. In these sentences the subject usually follows the verb and controls its number.

> There are many ways to fend off bankruptcy.

Generally speaking, only the first part of a compound subject following the verb in these sentences is used to determine the number of the verb.

> There is too much waste and inefficiency in this company.
> (verb)   (subj.)   (subj.)

Remember the agreement rules of *there* constructions, but try to use them sparingly. See p. 57–58.

toward/towards Dictionaries call *towards* "archaic and rare." Save it for an antique convention.

try and/try to Writing is more precise than speech. Although we may say—and hear—such a sentence as "She will try and pass the test," this is neither good nor proper language use. When we write that someone is *attempting* something, we do not mean that the person is both trying

TH–TR

and doing; we mean the person is trying *to* do something. It makes sense to introduce the infinitive with the preposition *to*.

She will try <u>to</u> pass the test.

unique This adjective begs to be adorned with superficial and redundant words, as in "most unique" or "very unique." Our advice: Snap out of it! *Unique* means, simply, "the only one of its kind." Don't succumb to word inflation or to an embarrassing overstatement that reveals a misunderstanding of meaning.

up It can be anything but upbeat when it is coupled with a verb. Cluttered phrases such as *face up, slow up* and *head up* just slow down meaning.

The administrator must <u>face up</u> to the inefficient situation in his department.
Why can't this administrator just *face* the inefficient situation?

See p. 134.

verb The verb is the heart and soul of a sentence. It breathes, sings, squeezes, inspires; it drives all the other sentence parts. When chosen correctly, it is in command. Pick your verbs wisely; they can take you far. Don't forget: You don't have a sentence without a verb that sets in motion a complete thought. See pp. 14–18.

verbals These constructions—participial phrases, infinitives and gerunds—sometimes have the feel of action, but that is mainly related to the *-ing* endings on many of them and to the apparent verb form that follows *to* in infinitives. Don't be confused; verbals do not control the movement of a sentence. They are really nouns, adjectives or, sometimes, even adverbs, as in

<u>Walking</u> through the fields of County Cork, she <u>discovered</u> a sleeping leprechaun. (The true verb is *discovered*. *Walking* is part of a participial phrase and is an adjective that modifies the personal pronoun *she*.)

very Be very wary of intensifying adjectives with *very*. If you get used to the practice, you might very well be overlooking very much better, more precise adjectives and contributing to clutter. *Very* is only one example of an overused intensifier. Others are *really, completely, extremely* and *totally*. For example, rather than describing someone as *very sad*, you could choose among these words: *depressed, melancholy, sorrowful* or *doleful*. See p. 152.

who's/whose If you want the contraction, use *who's*.

> **Who's speaking on the chicken dinner circuit tonight?** (Who is speaking . . .)

If you need the possessive pronoun, use *whose*.

> **Whose boat has been reported missing?** (To whom does that boat belong?)

If you want to use *whose*, it must modify something directly or by implication. In the preceding sentence, *whose* modifies *boat*.

who/whom Although colloquial speech has done its best to eliminate *whom* from this handsome pair of pronouns, the case for their survival together remains strong. In most writing situations the use of *whom* does not seem elitist; it is merely correct.

> **Whom did the president name to his cabinet?**

The use of *whom*, the objective case of *who*, shows the reader that the pronoun receives the action of the verb rather than initiates it. Similarly, avoiding the tendency to use the objective case improperly can show the reader that the action is beginning with the pronoun.

WH–YO

> **The jockey who the magazine said had thrown the race has been cleared by the state commission.**

An analysis of this sentence reveals that *who had thrown the race* is a subordinate clause and that *the magazine said* is for attribution only and not part of the key structure of the clause. Obviously, proper selection of *who* and *whom* shows that you are a writer who understands the function of sentence parts. If you also want to utter such sentences as "Whom did you wish to see?" when someone comes to your door, well, that's up to you.

your/you're The same distinctions given in the entries for *their/they're* and *who's/whose* apply here. If you want to use the possessive form of the personal pronoun *you*, use *your*.

> **Your Freudian slips are showing.** (*Your* modifies the noun *slips*.)

If you want to compress (contract) the subject-verb *you are*, use *you're*.

> **You're going to be a great grammarian!**

INDEX